The Legend • The Legacy

SHERMAN J. HOWARD:
Football and Beyond

●●●●

The Legend and Legacy of an
African-American NFL Pioneer

An autobiography as presented by:

VIETTA L. ROBINSON

Interior & cover layout & design:
Tarsha L. Campbell

Published by:
DOMINIONHOUSE
Publishing & Design
P.O. Box 681938 | Orlando, Florida 32868 | 407.703.4800
www.mydominionhouse.com

Acknowledgments & Dedication

GRACIAS, MERCI, TODAH!

I wish to acknowledge Nancy Butler-Ross, my first editor, who caught the vision immediately and passionately assisted in expanding my original transcript to so much more.

My high school friend, Sam Hogsette, showed up 40 years later as a College History Instructor and added some rich historical facts to my dad's journey.

My sister Yvette who is and always has been my biggest supporter.

Tarsha Campbell whose patience and professionalism is just what I needed to finally get this writing published.

****

This book is dedicated to my father and all other athletes who have trained and excelled despite the odds against them. They have influenced and inspired many observers near and far.

The wisdom on the pages that follow is invaluable. This book is not just about the early football experience but the courage, consciousness, and convictions revealed in my father's words. The first title for this book was It's Not About The Football, which, although motivating, quickly became inadequate...

TABLE OF CONTENTS

This extraordinary man, Sherman Howard, will come to life on the forthcoming pages and you will begin to understand and be inspired by events that both shaped and influenced him. Every part of this writing journey has brought me to love and appreciate my father more. I give you this book as a gift from me and the universe.

FOREWORD

I was so thrilled going through the draft of this book, as I was captivated by the life of Mr. Sherman Howard, particularly of the different eras of history, culture, and influences, not to mention the challenges he undertook and overcame throughout his life.

I met the author, Vietta Robinson, in 2009 and we are business partners to this day. I was just captivated by the fact that America is a melting pot of nations. Vietta comes from an American Indian and African lineage and I have my roots in Europe and Asia. We share common interests, such as health and the love of Abba (which is Hebrew for "Father").

What is so amazing about Vietta is that she learned so much from her father, Sherman Howard's experiences, and decided to write a book so the next generations would not miss the richness of his wisdom. I see her desire to be a great contributor and a world shaker, not only to her own family, but also to her community.

Vietta has made me a third-party onlooker, allowing me the ability to give my opinion and infuse the pages of this book with history revolving around the life of her dad and some of her ancestors to make it not just a great biography but a source of inspiration, a historical and cultural resource, and a powerful guide for others as they overcome the hurdles in their lives.

—Karen Owen

INTRODUCTION

L iving longer, healthier lives and anti-aging are frequently the main topics of 21st-century health conferences, which focus on the latest research and cutting-edge strategies, and ask audiences, "What are the keys to longevity?" I've often asked this question myself as I've observed my father and other seniors growing old with grace and wisdom. While there are many seminars, books and videos marketed to offer tools for living a long and healthy life, perhaps nature and those amazing people who have made it past the three-quarters of a century mark can provide the most insight and understanding about opening a path to longevity.

In nature, the mighty Mississippi River exemplifies longevity and integration with the landscape and human lives it touches as it carves its way through this country to the Gulf of Mexico. By the very nature of its presence, the Mississippi dynamically participates in the sculpting of culture, community, neighborhoods and neighbors along its shores, radiating for many miles inland.

As the "Great River" flows in straight and meandering patterns from Minnesota to Louisiana, it is joined by tributaries that integrate their energies and dramatically increase the Mississippi's strength, a process that has gone on for thousands of years, participating in the culture and dynamics of different neighborhoods. It reminds me of a journey and life I've been privileged to know and to write about with much excitement.

In much the same way as the Mississippi River, my father has moved through his life touching, sculpting, integrating and influencing those around him in ways far beyond what he may ever know. Nevertheless, he has made an indelible impact on individuals and changed countless lives.

In my father's life journey, integration was more of an assignment with challenges and conflicts at depths I have rarely experienced. The word "integration" can have a complex and deep meaning, depending on the context in which it is used. One event in particular has given me new insight into the significant roles my father and I are playing to bring awareness to the purpose and plan of our Creator.

In 1948, at the age of twenty-four, Sherman Howard, my father, became the first African-American to play college football in the "Jim Crow" city of Tulsa, Oklahoma. At that time, he was one of only two black men on the University of Nevada-Reno football team, a team newspapers reported had the best offense in the United States. His anticipated arrival in Tulsa for the game against the University of Tulsa generated much anxiety and questions, with one newspaper headline reading, "Set Precedent?"

According to local newspapers, fullback Sherman Howard, who scored touchdowns, blocked, and protected his quarterback, was the MVP of that game, as his contribution ensured a solid victory for his team, 65-14. But while it was the worst loss for the Tulsa team in 31-years, it was also the end of a generation of racial segregation, at least on that football field. It was a victory for the University of Nevada, but more importantly a major victory for racial integration, which was in motion even before my father's birth.

The first time I heard about this history-making game was in 2009 when I was fifty-four. I could probably attribute this to the fact that my father is not one to brag a lot, but if asked a question he will certainly have an opinion that could last for several minutes. While I remember all the football pictures that hung on the walls in the Chicago apartment where I grew up, the significance of those photos didn't register until I was much older. I was even more surprised to find that in 2010 football cards with my father's picture were trading on ebay for up to forty dollars each.

Early in 2009 I decided it was time to write my father's story. So I called my sister in Atlanta and we both agreed we should take a tape recorder and a list of questions to Chicago and record our father's words. He would turn eighty-five in November and this seemed like the right time to begin the writing process while his mind was clear. Plus my writing energy was still flowing since I had just completed my first self-published booklet. So in June 2009 my sister and I met at the Atlanta airport and headed for Chicago to record Sherman Howard's story, a story that includes his memories of the journey he made during what history now calls the Great Migration from the South to the North. My sister and I had performed a reverse migration, so to speak, by choosing to live in Georgia and Florida, respectively, for the last thirty years. Thanks to Daddy and his generation, Baby Boomers like my sister and me have more choices regarding where to live and work.

We had planned to spend three days interviewing my father at his home, asking questions and getting all the facts recorded. At the time, my father's three-year-old granddaughter was also visiting from Louisiana, so the first two days of our visit were busy chatting with relatives and doing other unplanned activities. It wasn't until about 10 or 11 p.m. on the third day we were in Chicago that we finally sat down at the kitchen table and began the interviewing process. That moment seemed to say it all, as three generations sat attentively listening for wisdom and insight. My oldest son was part of the third generation, as he had flown in the previous day to join us.

As we began asking my father questions, the three-year-old was banging a toy on the table. We continued anyway, trying to ignore her, with tape recorder rolling. Someone eventually directed her to another room and the interview continued with fewer distractions, at least until midnight when our scheduled visit would end.

On the third day of our visit, however, we all sat at that table, each relaying different perspectives about the past but carrying dreams, hopes, and visions for a prosperous future. Sherman Howard had not only planted the seed that allowed each of us to be there, but he had also lived a life that continued to nourish and bless his offspring.

Back home in Orlando, I began transcribing the tape. Several months later, after much procrastination, I had sixteen typed pages and loads of great pictures from my father's early football days. Listening to that tape later, even with a three-year-old's noise in the background, I realized how precious that moment was and how important it is to share my father's story. Although many know a general history of this country's segregation and African-American people's struggle for civil rights, I wonder how many understand what it takes to survive such a dark and challenging period.

My generation's health coaches, massage therapists, Yoga teachers and Reiki Masters are now preparing to minister much-needed healing from such a tumultuous time, as they gain the knowledge and experience necessary to return a sense of balance and well-being to emotionally and physically damaged warriors from the integration battlefield. Much like the Mississippi, we are now seeing the consequences of a journey filled with conflict, abuse and a draining of the soul.

I was only eight-years-old in 1963 when African-Americans all over the United States were participating in some of the most intense and violent demonstrations for equality. It has been estimated there were more than 1,000 civil rights demonstrations in a three-month period that year. My father viewed himself as having been involved in civil rights his entire life. He was able to adjust to any situation he found himself in where color was a factor without getting frustrated or trying to hurt anyone. He simply, "handled it in [his] own way." Most of the white people on his youthful path judged him for his excellent character, and the end result was usually positive. He simply laughed out loud when confronted with racist attitudes, even if he was cursing silently. Most blacks in a segregated society kept a subservient attitude for fear of losing their lives, their jobs, or even their rental homes since their landlords were usually white. My father's philosophical perspective, past and present was:

Black people have been acting all their lives. Nothing new. Most of the kids today don't know how to adjust to the civil rights problem. If you're walking down the street and you see a lion, you have to know what to do. You can't go up to him and argue with him. You have to try and figure out how to deal with him. Nowadays, kids go to drugs or wearing their pants below their belt as a protest, to let them know "I'm an individual." But that's not solving the problem.

My father taught me these types of lessons all my young life, even giving me food for thought because I had not been exposed to the turmoil many blacks were experiencing. My father's move north to the city of Chicago at an early age became somewhat of an oasis from the ignorance and poverty of the South, especially for his children. All his children attended college, and two of the four graduated. But most importantly we were trained to pay attention to important life lessons, the death of a child being one of the most profound.

The wisdom on the pages that follow is invaluable. This book is not just about the early football experience but the courage, consciousness and convictions revealed in my father's words. The first title for this book was *It's Not About The Football*, which, although motivating, quickly became inadequate. As I was writing this book, I began to understand how my father's early experiences shaped the relationships he had. The "coach," as he was called throughout his teaching years, continues to reflect, with amazing accuracy of details, the many events that shaped his character.

My sister and I consider ourselves blessed to have "Daddy" still around and hope everyone who reads this book will not just enjoy the pictures (they are awesome!) but also ask themselves the important question: "Will I play the 'human game' or the 'race game' when faced with conflicts in my life?" Playing the human game means trying to understand a person's behavior by paying attention to emotions, feelings and words in order to develop quality relationships.

The race game, on the other hand, has always been played out of ignorance and fear, with no desire to understand or change erroneous perceptions. Whichever game you choose to play, you will face some important consequences, and the time feels right to make huge progress toward spiritual consciousness, the place where we understand the energy behind thoughts, feelings, and emotions, which is key to changing our environment, both local and global. Once we understand and change our way of thinking, we can begin to experience that peace that passes all understanding.

At the age of ninety my father takes no medication, and although he moves at a slower pace than he did when he was younger, he still performs exercises at home to help his circulation. His kitchen cabinets are full of herbal teas and extracts, supplements and other health-sustaining products. Most of his close friends and former football associates are deceased, so occasional trips to the NFL conventions keep him closely informed of the business and current events in today's professional football arena.

I realize more and more how important it is to have conversations with our elders so we can gain wisdom and learn from their achievements as well as their mistakes. When I was younger I disagreed and argued with my dad frequently, but as wisdom has taken over, I love to listen, reflect, and as the Kabbalah saying goes, "Observe without judgment." This has helped me grow and develop healthy relationships with quality conversations of light and love that continue to inspire me. There is light and love in all of us; it just takes listening ears and eyes to seek the good and discern them. Plus, exercising patience influences what we reap from our seeds of love, which my father sowed regardless of the condition of the field. His story has and will continue to produce a harvest of enlightened and caring individuals. Longevity and wisdom speak if we will only listen.

This extraordinary man, Sherman Howard, will come to life on the forthcoming pages and you will begin to understand and be inspired by events that both shaped and influenced him. Every part of this writing journey has brought me to love and appreciate my father more. I give you this book as a gift from me and the universe. A messenger like Sherman Howard only comes once in a while, so it's important that we listen, take note and blossom where we are planted. This river of long life will flow into your heart and give you some assistance for the journey ahead.

In May 2011, while NFL players and owners were in contract talks, the *Chicago Tribune* interviewed Sherman Howard. The title of the interview was "Former player thinks current players worry too much about money." Of the twenty or more responses to the article, the one my father brought to my attention was a comment from "current NFL players," which simply stated "shut up, old man." That comment generated fifty-four thumbs down and sixteen thumbs up, so clearly the majority of readers did not agree with that comment. The comment that received an overwhelming sixty-one thumbs up and zero down was "Many players these days use their contracts as measuring sticks for their male appendages." Hmmm. So to those few professional athletes who may carry the "shut up" sentiment, reading Sherman's story could be the beginning of your longevity journey that could bring you to a position of being interviewed at the age of eighty-seven with a healthy mind, body and spirit. There is knowledge, understanding and wisdom to be gained. And nothing to lose.

WHAT PEOPLE ARE SAYING ABOUT MR. HOWARD

Coach Howard taught us how to play football, but more importantly he taught us how to be men. Men in the sense of living a life of hard work, values and integrity. We gave Coach Howard a nickname secretly (Sherm), but we had absolute love and respect for him. Coach Howard taught us lessons that have stayed with me to this day, i.e., "football is 20% talent and 80% effort," an insight that has been invaluable in both my personal and professional life. He has done a lot for me and other young men fortunate enough to play for him.

Michael Dennis Young, Ph.D.
(former student at Harlan High School, Illinois)
Vice Chancellor for Student Affairs
University of California, Santa Barbara

Young Sherman with his mother, 1934

The Legend • The Legacy

CHAPTER 1

EARLY YEARS FROM NEW ORLEANS TO CHICAGO

As early as 1879, blacks began moving northward, escaping lynch mobs and poor economic conditions to seek higher wages and better housing. When word came from the north that there was a better life for poor blacks living in the south, in the summer of 1934 in the midst of "The Great Depression," a young Sherman Howard and his mother traveled north by train to the Windy City, which would become their home for many years.

While the rest of the nation was concerned with job loss and the recent stock market crash, most black families were struggling with a continual depression of poverty and racism. Sitting in a segregated car without air conditioning, visually aware of the smoke from the train's engine, the 24-hour journey to Chicago gave my father plenty of time to reflect on his place of birth. Nicknamed "Crescent City" for its expansion along the curving Mississippi river, New Orleans was only the beginning of my father's continuing turning and expanding journey and ever-flowing opportunities.

As he remembers:

> My mother and I left New Orleans in 1934 when I was nine and in the third grade, heading to Chicago for a vacation. My stepfather worked on the railroad and he got us passes to go. I remember getting off the train at different stops like Memphis, and my mother couldn't read or write so I had to do all the reading for her. So you would get off the train and go over here and get off again and go over there. They were all segregated trains that gave us a different perspective of life away from home.

Sherman John Howard was born in the city of New Orleans to Loretta Moore and Johnny Howard on November 28, 1924, weighing in at thirteen pounds. Wow! Since Loretta and Johnny were not married, raising my father became the responsibility of his mother and her family. My father was born at a time and into a race of people whose daily thoughts were on survival. Daddy had one brother, Clarence, who was nine years his senior.

In terms of education and civil rights, Louisiana was one of the most backward states in the union. My father's mother couldn't read or write, and living in abject poverty, she later told Sherman, "I tried all sorts of things to keep from having you." Because in those days if a woman didn't want to have a child, she tried all sorts of "abortion" methods, including douches and coat hangers, not knowing how they would affect her body. So his mother didn't have any idea how to "properly" have an abortion. It's a sad reminder of the helplessness and desperation women in her situation felt.

Sherman's mother, my grandmother, died of ovarian cancer at the age of 38, which speaks to me of the struggles she had in her reproductive area. I never met my grandmother, but my father's memories of his mother have given me insight into her character and trials. At ninety, my father remembers events that took place some seventy-plus years ago because they left an imprint on his psyche. As a result, he put his mother's words in his memory bank and forged ahead to become a pioneer, carrying a much-needed banner of truth and sanity, which he later used to influence and inspire thousands of inner-city youth. I now realize my father's wisdom was inspired by his mother's continual positive outlook and a heart full of encouragement and love.

My own mother, Lillian, spoke to me before she passed about her thoughts of aborting me. Hearing that from your own mother can either make you very sad or cause you to reflect on the Divine hand that overrules a mother's thoughts and actions. So I was surprised, but not saddened, to hear those words. I could only look upward and say "thanks," just as my father has done so well his entire life. Sherman Howard carries absolutely no judgment toward his mother and believes abortion is an issue of consciousness or awareness of our Divine assignment. Healthy emotions and relationships are the keys to longevity, as my father has demonstrated so beautifully.

My father and his brother, Clarence, walked the dirt roads of New Orleans in the 1930s, often without shoes, and as my father put it, "You didn't have to worry about what you would wear tomorrow because you wore the same clothes every day." This early experience, along with similar experiences of lack, helped solidify my father's attitude of gratitude and appreciation for the many blessings that came later. For it was in his birthplace of New Orleans that he received a thorough education on survival, obedience, and submission to segregation laws.

I had always known my father spent his first eight years there, so I asked him, "Daddy, what was it like to live in the Deep South in the 1920s and early thirties?"

"It was a day-to-day struggle in New Orleans for most blacks, and New Orleans was well known for the red-light district in the French Quarter, where prostitution was very open in the 1920s," was his answer. He remembers hearing how black and white women prostituted themselves in the French Quarter, even though it was against the law. Algiers, the section where he grew up, was a port town where sailors would arrive and find the women they wanted: blacks, Creoles, Cajuns, and any other race of American women.

"There was only one hospital in the area and you had to take a ferry boat to get to it," Daddy said. "If someone had an emergency, it was a long wait sometimes for the ferry boat to return." Daddy and his brother were barefoot most of the time, ate pancakes and syrup frequently, and drank lemonade with sugar. Some people had a garden and grew their own food. His grandmother had one in her backyard, so she frequently cooked greens or cabbage, with salt pork, and ate beans at least twice a week with corn bread. "Folks did a lot of fishing and hunting for rabbits, squirrels and frogs for their food," my father stated. "You couldn't have any selective diet; you just ate what was available. The local farmers had fresh vegetables and fruit, but in the city there was no telling what you would eat." Daddy often told us he asked his mother many times "Are we eating?" instead of *"What* are we eating?"

In both New Orleans and Chicago, my father's environment as a child was often cold and lacking in basic needs, but these days when I visit Daddy's Chicago home in the winter, the temperature inside is always quite warm.

At the age of fifteen, nine years before Sherman came along, his mother gave birth to his only brother, Clarence. What Daddy remembers most about his mother is that she was very thoughtful, loving and kind, and always made sacrifices for him. She was a strong disciplinarian and when she told my father to do something, she meant "Do it *now.*"

To earn money, she would wash a whole basket of clothes for fifty cents, using a washing board and a pan underneath it to scald the sheets. After ironing them, Daddy would carry them to the customer in his wagon and he or she would pay the fifty cents. His mother was illiterate, so she couldn't read the streetcar signs. Daddy had to go everywhere with her to help her read and sign documents, especially after they moved to Chicago.

Music was part of their daily lives, as well. His mother had an old Victrola and played it all the time. Someone was always winding it too much, so it became Daddy's job to get it fixed. His mother grew up with musicians like Louis Armstrong, the famous trumpet player. Her sister even dated one of his band members.

Every Saturday night was party night, which included music and alcohol. My father has often told me his relatives drank alcohol on the weekends and even as a young boy he cleaned up the vomit and other messes they left behind. This continued even after they moved to Chicago. The people in his life didn't know how to take care of themselves, and witnessing the sickness and subsequent deaths of his mother and her relatives not only gave him reason to work hard to improve his life, but also started a passion in him to teach health and physical education. Two of the sisters, Aunt Julia and my grandmother, died just a few years after arriving in Chicago.

When I asked about my grandfather, Sherman's father, Daddy became pensive:

I slightly remember my father from when I was

about three or four or five. All I know is he died right before my mother did, in 1938. My mother was thirty-eight, my father [was] forty-one when they died. Out of the thirteen children in my father's family, eleven died early and only his sister, Aunt Evelyn, survived to an old age. When they got sick, they didn't have any doctors.

My father worked as a stevedore on the docks in New Orleans, unloading ships. He loaded one-hundred-pound bales of cotton, day in and day out, all day long for fourteen hours. That's a lot of work. He would go to work at six in the morning and come home at eight at night. You go to work at night and come home at night and get ready to go to work again. By the time you eat, it's time to go to work again.

If you had kids they all slept on the floor. They couldn't sleep in beds. Pallets were made of rolled-up blankets, and you slept on the floor. Sleeping on the floor had its risk when chickens were in the house. We would keep chickens in the kitchen to keep thieves from stealing them outside.

Daddy never slept in a regular bed the first eighteen years of his life, nor did he have three meals a day until he served in the military. He slept on the kitchen floor and covered his head to keep the chickens from pecking at it. A very cautious and somewhat fearful attitude toward birds remains with him even at age eighty-five. Just getting a good night's sleep in a comfortable bed is something he treasures.

> In those days, as soon as a girl in the house got mature enough to bear kids, they would try and find her a husband to get her out of the house. We had one big room with curtains separating the bedroom area. I remember vaguely seeing my father, but I never really saw my father much at all. My mother would say, "Go see your dad; he might give you something." I couldn't tell you exactly what he was like. It was never that type of close relationship where I spoke to him often or spent time with him.

> In those days guys might stay with their [wives] awhile; then they would go somewhere else. It wasn't that bond they have now because it was such a hard life for a man to just try and survive, especially in 1924 in New Orleans. A

child didn't even have to go to school until 1924 because they passed the compulsory attendance law in 1924. They didn't back it up with people who made sure you go to school. In other cities they had a law and they made sure you went to school. They just passed a law to make it look good. Nobody checked to see if you did go.

Louisiana was one of the worst states in the U.S. at that time. They had several racial divisions: French, whites, Creoles, mulattos, [and] Cajuns. Blacks were the last group they catered to and they would just ignore the blacks and cater to the other groups. They had four different groups that were ahead of you. Blacks didn't have any political clout so the only challenges were the other groups.

The Catholic Church would help the blacks, sort of like missionary work. They knew they had so many bodies. They were not real educators but disciplining of the pilgrim type. "Do what I say" or you would get your butt whipped; therefore, I started out in the Catholic school kindergarten, but my mother did not agree with all that whipping. So she put me in the public school when I was about seven or eight.

The segregated school Daddy went to in the Algiers section of New Orleans housed first to twelfth grades in one building. The city built schools for the whites, the mulattos, and the Creoles before they built them for the blacks. Daddy remembers his school by the number "32" because of the succession of schools built from a specific fund. A millionaire and slaveholder by the name of John McDonough had specified in his will that his money was to be used for the education of the whites and the free blacks. Although my father didn't complete his early education in New Orleans, the memory of one of the first decent school buildings for blacks is fresh in his memory seventy-seven years later. When I asked him if he remembered any childhood friends or classmates, however, he could not recall any. He spent most of his time helping his mother and other adults, leaving little time for play or school activities.

After teaching in the Chicago public schools for 30 years, Daddy explained:

That's why the European education system was so far ahead of ours. They didn't prolong adolescence like we do. And the labor unions are the cause of that. They didn't want the young people coming out of school and getting jobs. But at one time in the 1920s and thirties they didn't have that job problem because there was always a shortage of labor. But when they started unionizing, the union workers wanted to make sure they had job[s] and they prolonged the guys coming out of high school until they were eighteen-years-old.

When my father was a child in Louisiana, he paid close attention to the daily interaction between adults of all races. They "would be around one another," he said, "but they had the social structure where blacks couldn't do this or that."

He remembers the restrictions placed on his own relatives as well as the freedom exercised by those with lighter skins. Movie theaters had side entrances for blacks to enter and they were only allowed in the balconies. "Jim Crow" was alive and well, as most department stores and restaurants banned blacks, and there were also segregated restrooms and schools. I can picture him with eyes wide open looking at the sea of colored faces and ears listening to the voices he encountered in the heat and humidity of New Orleans.

Amid the tumultuous signs of division, fear and ignorance, he recognized at a very young age that racism was indeed a strange game. It must have been both entertaining in some respects and yet puzzling, as his mother continued to remind him, "They [white folks] have the problem, not us."

Interestingly enough, the conversations the people around him engaged in revealed an interesting blood connection between whites and blacks. As my father recalls, "You start talking to them and often discover that we're all related." Even as a child, Sherman began to understand that Miss Jackson, a mulatto woman, was related to Mr. Smith, a white man and Miss Annie, a black woman, was a distant cousin of Miss Sarah, a white woman.

Society was separated by what now seems to be a ridiculous categorization of people: Mulattos, Creoles, and blacks of various shades of skin that were distinguished from one another. My father recalls from his studies that when the United States took over the territories from France in 1803 as part of the "Louisiana Purchase," it created what was considered "a big problem in New Orleans." Whites were immediately elevated to a higher economic and social status, while the Creoles, the mulattos, and blacks were relegated to a lower socio-economic status. Long after slavery had officially ended, it would be a much longer time before the defeat of segregation and the advent of integration.

With such a beautiful mixture of races and cultures in New Orleans, one might think changing racial attitudes would be relatively easy, but change comes slowly to the spiritually blind. Without a doubt, my father's upbringing in New Orleans greatly influenced his life and subsequent actions.

My father gazed at the world through Divine eyes. As he grew, he focused on athletic games rather than the race game of ignorance, jealousy, hatred and violence. Running steadily through the racism game, he confronted the hurdles of segregation to effectively interact with and influence people of all races, and carried on to score touchdowns on and off the field. Even though he nearly died before he was born, his earthly assignment was destined to be successful. His near-death experience in the womb reminds me of men like Moses, Joseph, and even Christ, who triumphed over death and made a difference in their time. As the battle continued into the twentieth century, the time and season were ripe for pioneers, warriors, standard-bearers and messengers to break through the darkness of racism with a torchlight of love and truth.

My father recounted his life-changing vacation to Chicago: "So finally we arrived in Chicago, and my Aunt Julia met us. I was to live in Chicago with my mother and another stepfather. Our short vacation turned into many years, we never went back to New Orleans and Aunt Julia died in 1936."

Although early migrators paved the way for improved housing, schools and social services that benefited my father's generation and beyond, when my father arrived in Chicago, there were many socio-economic challenges. On a positive note, the sound of jazz music and the smell of Gumbo, a flavorful Louisiana soup that includes okra, vegetables, shrimp and other meats, were being heard and tasted throughout the north, giving hearts and bodies some much-needed warmth and comfort. As one writer put it, "Chicago replaced New Orleans as jazz's happening city during the 1920s. Musicians from New Orleans and elsewhere in the South gravitated toward the rapidly growing Windy City, where bustling clubs and recording studios gave the players a shot at national notoriety."[1]

Part of the reason my father was able to survive as a young person growing up in Chicago was the lunches the school system provided to kids. My father observed:

> Most blacks were on welfare and the jobs were day-labor jobs, which meant a day-to-day struggle to provide life's essentials. There were neither black bus drivers nor city train drivers. We would pick up clothes at the welfare stations that President Franklin Roosevelt instituted. Day-labor jobs included car washing for three dollars. The unions were tightly controlled with the result that both northern as well as the newly arrived uneducated blacks from the South were excluded from the unions and unable to find much more than service jobs.

> In Chicago, some men could attend a trade school at 16 and earn an apprenticeship license. But no blacks could ever get one, because you had to be recommended by another union member. Moreover, no blacks knew another union member because they were excluded from the unions.

Daddy continued to explain, insightfully:

The jobs at the post office and Pullman porters were some of the few lucrative jobs available to blacks. See, 90 percent of the blacksmiths and carpenters before and after the Civil War were black. Who do you think built all those plantations? Who paved those roads? Who built the White House? There weren't many white laborers during slavery. Slaves did all the work. Now all the people who were blacksmiths were good enough to build all these houses, but as soon as they freed the slaves, they were unemployed.

So what happened? Daddy continues:

They opened immigration to additional Europeans and advertised for labor and skills. They came to the United States by the thousands. They might get here today and they had a job tomorrow. You stay here all your life and you couldn't get a job. The Irish and Italians caught hell. No Irish, no blacks, no Italians. That's why I always say this is not a Christian nation. Never has been. Sure, the United States had more than a few Christians, but given their actions, [it] cannot rightfully be a Christian nation. Why? Because they always exploited the underdog to make a profit. And now, right now, that same thing is still going on.

His older brother, Clarence, left the family home in New Orleans when he was fourteen and my father saw very little of him until Clarence moved to Chicago. Sherman says of his older brother:

> Clarence got a girl pregnant and in those days if you got someone pregnant, you had to get out of the house. Clarence attended school up to the fifth grade, so he was able to read and write. That was the big thing if you could read and write. Since there were no child labor laws in Louisiana, if Clarence could find a job shining shoes on a ferry boat going across, he could make some money.

Clarence married his first and second wives in Louisiana, but like my father, he spent most of his life in Chicago. Clarence stayed in New Orleans until the 1940s, at which time he moved to Chicago with his son, Craig, and his third wife.

When Clarence went to Chicago, he was hired by International Harvester, a farm equipment company. It wasn't long, however, before he experienced unemployment because the workers went on strike frequently.

But Clarence's attitude was, "I'm tired of being on strike; I want to work every day."

In fact, my father proudly told me:

> Even though American Airlines had a hiring freeze at the time, your Uncle Clarence went to their employment office and made a plea to work for them. They recognized his character; he was hired as a plane cleaner and he worked for the company until his retirement many years later.

Uncle Clarence was one of only a handful of relatives on my father's side of the family that I remember visiting occasionally. He eventually moved to Texas with his wife and son. After he and his wife died, however, we lost contact with his son.

Since my paternal grandmother married several men and Daddy had multiple stepfathers, I always wondered how he felt growing up without a consistent male role model in the house. Today, many women face the challenge of single parenthood due to a variety of circumstances. As my father discovered, however, that challenge can be overcome when men become mentors in their communities. I asked my father which men in his life had influenced him the most. He replied:

Now Mr. Walker was my stepfather when we moved to Chicago and he would get day work. He would paint a house or simonize cars for five dollars. Simonize and clean it for five dollars. And that was the type of work he did. He would take me to work with him every now and then to help clean, but that was survival. We came to Chicago in 1934 and my mother died in 1938. After she died, I started living with Aunt Vicey. That was only four years, but it seemed like a long time. When you're going through hell, each day [is] rough.

I had a lot of surrogate fathers. They would tell me basic things like, "Whatever you do in life, prepare like you're going to be at the White House. Whatever you're running, prepare like you're going to be in the Olympics. Playing football, play like you're going to be in the NFL. Basketball, like you are going to be the best. Never plan to stay at a low level." That's the type of guys I would meet. I remember when I was a kid in New Orleans, there was a baseball park and Satchel Paige was pitching to us kids. That was about ten years before he signed with the Cleveland Indians and became great.

We saw lots of sports figures in the neighborhood. Jack Johnson, the first black heavyweight-boxing champion, used to come in the playground. He used to tell us, "Do something with your life." Paul Robeson, the famous baritone singer and actor, among other things, was the same way. He'd say,

"Make your life worthwhile, so when you die somebody will say, 'Who was that?' There is always room for a good person. Go look for a job now; there's always room for a good person. Believe and they will see you're a different person."

All the men in my life came from outside— in the playground. Playground directors. My stepfathers were busy working, trying to survive. Back in those days you had day work. There weren't any steady jobs. Post office and Pullman porters were the only steady jobs. Guys who were fortunate enough to have these jobs made sure to keep it in the family to take them into the profession. It was those blacks and a few others who managed to establish something through the years.

Nevertheless, for the majority of blacks there was no avenue for anything. You could not get a job on the bus because they did not hire blacks. If you were lucky, the stockyard might hire a few. The unions controlled most of the jobs and they were reserved for whites. The shops were closed and filled with the relatives they would bring in.

There were many immigrants coming from Europe. The Germans, English and Jews took over everything. Blacks were last on the totem pole. There was nothing for you. You might go down to the coal company and they'd have you doing the heavy labor of unloading the coal off the trucks and you would go out with your shovel and in those days you would shovel the coal off the truck into where it was landing. That was your day's work. A man like Mr. Beaty, my best friend's dad, would get me a summer job working at Vienna sausage. I rode with a white truck driver as his helper, making deliveries to various stores every day.

I lived with Aunt Vicey for four years after my mother died. I graduated from grade school in January 1939, and Mr. Payton, our landlord who happened to be black, gave me his suit to wear. It was the first suit I ever wore. I didn't wear a suit again 'til I graduated from high school, four years later. Then I bought my own suit, a tailor-made suit for twenty-three dollars.

When my father mentioned his high school graduation, the name of his school, Wendell Phillips, came to my mind right away. I had heard that name many times growing up because my mother also attended Phillips High. Although the school opened in 1904 with a predominately white student body, by 1920 it had become the first predominately black high school in Chicago. From 1916 to 1919, an estimated 50,000 blacks moved to Chicago from the south, contributing to the city's fast-changing demographics. Chicago became "My Kind of Town" for thousands of blacks seeking change from their extreme poverty.

Many famous blacks, including recording artist Dinah Washington; Gwendolyn Brooks, the first black person to win the Pulitzer Prize; singer and jazz pianist Nat King Cole; and several men who played with the Harlem Globetrotters basketball team, were part of the Wendell Phillips alumni. In fact, from the 1920s on, Phillips produced many athletes who went on to play on college, semi-professional and professional teams.

When I asked my father what shaped or influenced his choice to play high school sports, I was not at all surprised at his answer:

> The great athletes I was surrounded by. I was surrounded by great basketball players. At that time, football was not as much a part of my life as basketball because basketball was acceptable to everybody. But you had restrictions with football. There were very few pro football players and very few guys around who actually played football. But there were a lot of basketball players. Many a great one.

> Now I ran track, too. We had many great trackmen around. So I ran track and played basketball except for my last year when I played football. You couldn't play football and basketball at the time I was in school. You had to play one or the other because the seasons were overlapping each other. Football went to the end of November, but basketball started in the first part of November. They limited your play to either football or basketball.

> Besides sports, I did have a couple of summer jobs. There was a national youth program for

kids in high school where you could earn four dollars a month working in the schools. That was during the war, around 1941.

Daddy had to grow up fast. His lessons in survival literally began on the playgrounds of Chicago and continued to the battlefields of Europe. After the battlefield, however, he was presented with some interesting opportunities to further compete in more than one sport.

Sherman Howard, High School Athlete

WHAT PEOPLE ARE SAYING ABOUT MR. HOWARD

As my teacher, mentor and football coach for the years 1961-1964, Mr. Howard instilled in me a sense of dedication to hard work and fair play. He nurtured my teammates and me with skill and patience. The teamwork and comradery instilled by Mr. Howard, coupled with his skillful and creative coaching, which was clearly influenced by his professional football experience, resulted in a cohesive, effective team, and we reversed our previous season's win-loss record. We went on that season to compete for the Chicago Blue Division championship. It was an invaluable experience to me and, I am certain, to my teammates.

Walter Ermler, Ph.D.
Professor of Chemistry
University of Texas at San Antonio

Sherman, you're in the Army now.

The Legend • The Legacy

CHAPTER 2

FROM THE BATTLEFIELD TO THE FOOTBALL FIELD

A t the age of eighteen, Sherman Howard was drafted into the U.S. Army. Like all U.S. soldiers, Daddy received filling meals, as well as shots against disease, so his general health and nutrition were good. Even though he often slept in the rain when he was in the service, he never even caught a cold. Tragically, however, the war left many of the veterans he got to know and love, to fight against the ravages of wartime disease.

One such veteran and close friend was Mr. Ferguson, who suffered almost forty years with complications of malaria, which progressively destroyed his lungs. A succession of doctors and treatments was unable to arrest the disease and Mr. Ferguson ultimately succumbed to it. Watching his friend (and relatives) suffer for many years helped shape Daddy into the humble man he is today.

Whether participating in the war at home or abroad, he garnered important lessons about life's essential battles of survival.

World War II, an international military conflict, lasted six years, from 1939-1945. White, Black, Asian, Native, and Hispanic Americans participated in that war, either on the front-lines or in supportive roles, as was the case of many black troops. Participation in war requires disciplined men and women to execute the orders issued by their superior officers. Soldiers who serve their country, whether as draftees or volunteers, deserve respect and honor for risking their lives on or near the battlefield.

Unfortunately, racial discrimination affected the treatment received by black men who served in World War II and other previous conflicts, even though they served honorably throughout the war in segregated units commanded by white officers. The color of a man's skin determined the respect and equality he received, which indicated the need for movement toward racial equality and social justice.

On December 19, 1945, my father and the black men he served with were scheduled to return to the United States.

Their homeward-bound journey, which should have been a relatively trouble-free trip, was unnecessarily troubled. The troops were assigned to travel aboard the U.S.S. Philadelphia (CL-41); however, the U.S. Commander of the Philadelphia refused to allow "negroes" to transport aboard his ship. Ironically, this was the same vessel where 15 black mess men wrote an open letter protesting their treatment in the Navy in September 1940. These men were subsequently jailed and given dishonorable discharges. This incident and others led to a series of meetings between civil rights leaders A. Phillip Randolph, Walter White, and President Franklin D. Roosevelt over the conditions blacks faced in the Armed forces, which resulted in the opening of black employment in the war industries.

As if the indignity of being denied transport on the Philadelphia was not enough, the weather added physical suffering to the emotional trauma returning servicemen experienced. The military newspaper, *Stars and Stripes*, wrote that it was an embarrassing situation for the United States. Yes, it was an embarrassment heightened by the fact that U.S. service members were transported home on an Argentine vessel. The mental and emotional succumbed to the physical when my father and everyone on that Argentine ship experienced incredibly severe weather, complete with towering seas, and at least four separate Atlantic storms with winds of eighty to one-hundred miles per hour. That rough ride back to the U.S. was a precursor of the storms that would ultimately challenge my father to trust in an internal strength and purpose galvanized by his experiences.

The Atlantic return crossing was such a rough conclusion to his wartime experience that it led me to ask my father, "If the ending was so traumatic, what was the war like?"

He replied:

> In 1943, World War II was still going on and I was drafted or "conscripted" as they called it. I served in a segregated unit called Port Battalion, and like most blacks [I] was assigned duties in transportation units. We would unload various ships removing guns, trucks, tanks and other cargo because in the countries where we were stationed, both England and France did not have enough young men to unload the ships, so they primarily used soldiers.
>
> Including basic training, we were stationed in the States for half a year, and then for two-and-a -half

years we were in Europe unloading supplies. Liverpool, England was our first posting and then later we moved to Manchester. After VE-Day (Victory in Europe) we went to Cherbourg, France, followed by LeHavre. We were around the places where battles had been fought, but in my service, I was never involved in a wartime battle. In other words, we were in the area but not on the front-line. There were definitely blacks on the front-line, but not my unit.

Perhaps being on the front-line would have given my father a different perspective regarding the racial inequality he would encounter in the U.S. Rather than battling in the bloody horror of war, however, he battled men carrying a ball instead of a gun. I will always believe the two battle stars he received were destined to be not just for his service in the European theater, but for the racial injustice he would experience.

Daddy recalls:

I played football in the service. Right after the war in Europe, General Dwight Eisenhower started a Special Service Division, which included baseball, football, track and basketball.

I played football, basketball and ran track under that program. In June 1945, I ran track in a "G.I. Olympics" in London.

Many people believe sports can help break down racial barriers more effectively than government interventions. This was certainly the case in Europe after World War II where all the teams were composed of men of various ethnic and racial backgrounds. For a brief moment in time in 1945, the battlefield consisted simply of leather balls and muscle power. While the Armed Forces remained segregated, in war-ravaged Europe was an integrated athletic program taking place prior to de-mobilization.

The end of the war brought opportunities to interact with other men on the athletic playing field regardless of the color of their skin. It was the military's command to return home that disrupted the semi utopia of sports-related integration and racial harmony, bringing a wake-up call to return to the good ole U. S. of A., where battles for racial equality and social justice were increasing.

After the dislocation of wartime service and the not-too-distant Great Depression, benefits for all returning U.S. soldiers were sorely needed. Many such benefits came from the Servicemen's Readjustment Act of 1944, commonly referred to as The G.I Bill. This bill extended low-interest mortgages; business loans; as well as tuition and living-expense payments for vocational, high school or college education. Most GIs, including my father, took full advantage of the educational benefits contained in that bill. This son of the south was now setting his sights on a college education.

My father had many mentors, but one in particular directed him, along with his friend, Earl Banks, to his first college, the University of Iowa in 1946. "Judge" Duke Slater was the first black All-American at Iowa, and after graduation he played ten years of professional football in the 1920s. Slater became an Assistant D.A. in Chicago in 1948 and later a judge. My father summed up his first college experience in this way:

> With the G.I. Bill you could go to any school you wanted; however, Iowa in the mid 1940s was prejudiced. Blacks couldn't get a haircut in Iowa City and you couldn't stay in the dorm.

> The athletic department, as far as the football team goes, only allowed one black in the backfield at a time, and my white team members were prejudiced. The athletics department had

a policy that would not allow blacks to play basketball. Moreover, off the field there was anger and resentment toward white girls talking to us. I recall being in a conversation with a friend who was a very popular white girl named Betsy, when a white guy rudely interrupted the conversation. She told him "Don't you see I'm talking?" Several whites resented the fact that Betsy was bold enough to publicly chastise a white man in the presence of a black; however, she was very popular, and was the President of the college council. One of her friends told me later that someone wrote "nigger lover" on her mirror.

There was dangerous anger all over the country regarding black men talking to or interacting with white girls. That was just one particular incident. I was just very sensitive to it, coming back from the war, fighting the war and all like that. I said to myself that for right now I wouldn't pay any attention to it.

While the All-American, Duke Slater, spent four years at the University of Iowa in the early twenties, Army veteran Sherman Howard was not going to endure four years there.

So in 1946, sensing an increasingly hostile environment, my father decided to search for a different college. The next stop was Los Angeles in the summer of 1947 where favor and Divine guidance would eventually lead him to Nevada.

I asked him how he got the chance to go to school in Nevada:

> Well, I was interested in attending this very famous school, known as UCLA, but UCLA would not accept the twelve hours of credit[s] I had accumulated at Iowa. So I was going to come back home to Chicago and continue my studies in health and physical education; however, while I was in Los Angeles, I had occasion to meet Herman Hill, a sports writer and editor of a black newspaper called the *Pittsburgh Carrier*. Herman contacted the University of Nevada and then told me to enroll there. That opened the door for me to move to Nevada.

His move to Nevada was also sweetened by the fact that Joe Sheetetski, the line coach from Iowa, was now head coach there.

I asked Daddy how the University of Nevada was different from Iowa. He replied:

Nevada was very open-minded and friendly. Most of my white Nevada teammates came from New Jersey, Pennsylvania, or California. Many were veterans of World War II and several of them grew up and played with blacks in their neighborhoods. We were like a big and close family. The girls would pick us up and take us to the parties. A woman who was the head of a sorority told me, "I made sure the girls danced with you."

Daddy continued:

There were no relationships at all, just knowing who the girls were and speaking to them. That was the extent of my involvement with the girls. I experienced absolutely no romantic or friendship relationships at all, just speaking in class. That's all. I had close relationships only with the guys I played ball with.

I also asked him what his relationships were with black women at that time. He replied:

There weren't any black women on Nevada's campus. The University of Iowa had a few but they commuted back and forth. There may have been two or three black girls there. At that time, I was not involved with any girls. I wasn't thinking about girls. I'd been to war and was glad to be home and had other things on my mind.

I was surprised to hear my father, a handsome man, say he had no time for women. Yet it helped me understand just how serious he took the opportunity to perform at his best and to make a difference on this integrated team. Sherman Howard, Army veteran and college football player, channeling his energy into practice and study, was destined to give an athletic performance that would amaze the people of Tulsa, Oklahoma, first, and later assist in advancing the cause of racial equality.

The University of Nevada's "Wolf Pack" football team was to play the Golden Hurricanes of the University of Tulsa on October 23, 1948. The Wolf Pack was not only rated the "Nation's Number 1 Offensive Team" but was one of the nation's few integrated college teams. Saturday the 23rd would be the first time "Negroes" would play football at Tulsa's Skelly stadium.

This contest between the Wolf Pack and the Golden Hurricanes became more than a typical college football game. It coincided with a delicate time of transition and awakening as a different battle was fought in Oklahoma. A civil rights struggle occurred at the same time over integrating white university classrooms in defiance of Oklahoma's segregation laws.

Even before the Wolf Pack arrived, newspaper headlines reflected the civil rights controversy and questions arising over this game. The *Tulsa Tribune* asked, "Is it legal for the University of Oklahoma to draw an 'invisible line' around its first Negro student, George W. McLaurin?" Famous attorney, Thurgood Marshall, was leading that battle in the courtroom while football coaches were respectfully discussing the possibilities for the upcoming game.

Two days prior to the game, the President of Tulsa University, Dr. C.I. Pontius, made the following statement:

> There is no clause in the contract between the University of Tulsa and Nevada University which would prevent the playing of any bonafide member of the Nevada football squad. The University of Tulsa will abide by this contract; however, the University of Nevada is aware of the traditional background of intercollegiate athletics in the state of Oklahoma and the decision with regard to playing

any member of its squad is the prerogative of the University of Nevada.

This left the decision about whether the two Negro players could play totally up to Joe Sheetetski, coach of the Wolf Pack, who had commented beforehand: "I want to make it plain that Nevada is not making any rash statements about this issue.... If we learn in Tulsa that Howard and Tabor can't play, that will end the matter." With full authority to make the decision, Coach Sheetetski and his thirty-five players boarded a plane for Tulsa, accompanied by Dr. John Moseley, President of the University of Nevada.

The Tulsa Daily World and several other newspapers captured my father's picture as he alighted from the plane. The headlines read: "Nevadans Have Rough Trip— No Decision on Negros"; "Coach Won't Say Who'll Play or Warm The Bench"; and my favorite, "Wolves Come In By Air."

The fact that several players were airsick from an "extremely rough trip" was reminiscent of my father's rough trip home after World War II. Three years later, flying into Tulsa with a team of mostly white men showed a degree of progress toward racial parity in accommodations if not yet in other areas. It seemed as if the heavens were preparing to reverse a cycle of hatred and suffering by rewarding a team that practiced love and chose to integrate.

Historically, Tulsa, Oklahoma was the site of one of the worst racial scenes against blacks in American history. Its black community was commonly known as the "Black Wall Street," and in 1921 became the target of a bloody assault by whites that, according to one official in the *Encyclopedia of Oklahoma History and Culture*, caused between fifty-six and three hundred deaths, and destroyed more than one thousand buildings, both private residences and businesses. An Internet report citing a book edited by John Hope Franklin and Scott Ellsworth, titled *The Tulsa Race Riot*, stated, "This riot was a horror never to be forgotten, a mark of shame upon the city that would endure forevermore."

Jim Crow legislation in Oklahoma not only aimed at keeping blacks from voting, but it also included a statute that made Oklahoma "the first state in the union to segregate its telephone booths." Fast forward to 1948 when my father was part of the University of Nevada football team and Jim Crow Laws were still in effect. Racial stereotypes, along with deeply ingrained racist attitudes and behaviors were still alive and well in Oklahoma. On

October 23, 1948, however, one man would break that law with the support of his coach and team. Sherman Howard was a necessary catalyst to changing the programming of hate and prejudice that had produced death, destruction, and more hatred for far too long.

The University of Nevada website describes that event as follows:

> The Nevada football team went on the road and defeated Tulsa 65-14, the Golden Hurricane's worst loss in thirty-one years. The victory was not the only significant occurrence that day, as Nevada became the first integrated team to play in the State of Oklahoma in defiance of that state's Jim Crow laws. Nevada coach Joe Sheetetski started African-American fullback Sherman Howard in the game. Howard went on to score a pair of touchdowns in the game, while backup quarterback Alva Tabor also passed for a touchdown.

Sherman Howard and Al Tabor were the only two blacks on the University of Nevada-Reno's football team and the first blacks to compete in college football in Oklahoma. At that time, Jim Crow laws in Oklahoma stated that blacks had to use separate public facilities, including water fountains, restrooms, and restaurant tables. Looking back, it seems strange that people came up with such laws, but when fear and ignorance are the predominant mindsets in a society, segregation and hatred seem to rule.

In sports, however, the rigid racial barriers began to fall. My father's performance in Tulsa that day won him the praise and admiration of many, causing athletic teams to rethink their segregated policies for victory's sake. As one newspaper described Daddy's performance, he would be considered the MVP by today's sports standards:

> Fullback Sherman Howard, the first Negro to ever play in Skelly stadium, was the only real runner on the Nevada team Saturday, but he spent most of the afternoon doing a terrific job of blocking and protecting Heath on passes…. The Nevada line gave Heath so much protection, he would have been able to tie his shoe laces before each toss….[2]

I asked my father how he adjusted to playing in a Jim Crow state. He replied:

> I always had to deal with Jim Crow laws. I made the adjustments necessary to allow me to

perform whatever task I needed to in those Jim Crow states. They had the problems, not me. I was taught early by my mother that white folks had the problem. I had no fears. I ignored the racial slurs. I had heard many times: "There's a nigger in the wood pile." Moreover, these people would tell me, "If all Negros were like you we'd be all right." Now the ultimate compliment was "I would let you marry my sister."

The Nevada coach asked if I wanted to play, and my teammates said they wouldn't play if I didn't play. We had a strong working relationship that was held together with courage, integrity and cooperation. Yes, there was name-calling from the stands, but I did not pay attention to the crowd. Jim Finks was the quarterback on the other team at that time. He later played pro football and spoke to me years later to let me know he didn't have the same prejudices as his team members.

I asked where he stayed when he traveled with the team. Daddy replied:

There was always a prominent black in the city who would house the blacks on the team. I recall there was a family that had oil wells in the back of their house. Black players were treated like family and as such, would have family dinners with them. Later, when I played in the pros, there was a special table reserved in the kitchen of these homes for the black pro players.

If I had stayed in Reno after graduation, I could have gotten anything I wanted. Why? Because the people I played with became successful businesspersons and civic leaders. William Morris, who played Center on the team, was on the board of trustees at the University of Nevada, and another teammate became a judge in Las Vegas. This is just two of many who did very well for themselves.

My son, Jibri, asked Daddy who he was close to on the team. His reply was swift:

All the guys on the Nevada team were real close. All of us looked out for one another. There was not a person on the entire team who would not do [his] best for you. The man who pushed me to be in the University of Nevada Hall of Fame became a millionaire.

While visiting Daddy at home in Chicago, I browsed through the latest University of Nevada yearbook. I knew very little of my father's experiences while he attended school there, so after I read about his coach, I asked Daddy to tell me what he thought about him. "He was an opportunist," Daddy said. "If he found someone who could help him do what he wanted to do, which was win games, then he used them. Blacks had the athletic and physical skills to help them win."

Daddy continued speaking very passionately:

> This whole thing with the black players made possible the changes in the athletic programs that we have today. It's not that they love blacks so much. These black players help win games and make money. That is the motivation. That is the reason; those black players bring in that money and help them win games!

Daddy continued with strong emotion:

> These are not great coaches; however, these are definitely great players! I made a decision after three years of education. I had attended the University of Iowa for one year, and then Nevada

for two, so I decided I was going to come back home to Chicago, work, and get a degree in teaching; however, before I could do this, I was drafted by the then New York Yanks of the NFL. They would later become the New York Giants of the All American Conference. The Yanks played in Yankee Stadium and they paid decent money, so I decided to go into professional football and play with the Yanks team.

The life of Sherman Howard, army veteran, student and athlete was markedly different from the life of most of the blacks in the late 1940s. While many blacks were experiencing hardships and racial repression, he was insulated because his white teammates at the University of Nevada were conscious and caring. This oasis from the prevailing mood in America at the time allowed him to shift from survival mode to thriving mode as he concentrated on his athletic, academic and relationship-building skills.

My father started his professional football career with the New York Yanks in 1949. While playing football with the New York Yanks, and later with the Cleveland Browns, Daddy's traveling experience was somewhat more comfortable than that of his teammates because when he played away games, he occasionally slept and dined in the homes of wealthy people of color, while his teammates had to settle for the dubious comforts of hotels.

The year 1949 was a very special year in the life of Sherman; it was the year he married my mother. Even though his combined college and professional football careers were relatively brief (six years), they gave him the experience he needed to teach health and physical education in the Chicago public schools.

A knee injury in 1953 convinced him to retire from professional football in 1954, but a new career called "family" not only kept him shifting and running to carry the weight of children and domestic challenges, but it also allowed him to complete his college degree. Needless to say, those five seasons he spent away from home as a professional football player put a strain on his marriage. I have come to understand why my mother thought of aborting me, her third child. No doubt my arrival brought more challenges for a woman struggling to maintain balance in her roles as wife and mother.

The Divine assignment to carry a banner for positive change offers much in the way of protection. My father obviously had many angels who rendered him invaluable assistance along life's pathways. Whether on the field of life or on the football field, Sherman Howard was always in training.

Sherman (2nd from rear) in WW II sports team.

University of Nevada-Oklahoma Game, 1948

****

A Glimpse from the Past
Quote from *Jet* Magazine

Sterling play by two of their Negro backs enable the non-winning, pro football New York Yankess to tie the San Francisco 49ers 10-all, in Yankee Stadium. Sherman Howard bolted 11 yards in the final quarter to score a touchdown.

12/6/51, pg. 26

Army, Brussels, Belgium, 1944

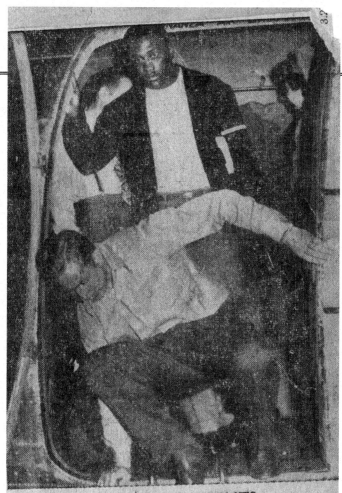

SET PRECEDENT?

Varsity Fullback Sherman Howard prepares to follow his
versity of Nevada teammate, Tackle Floyd Barqer of Perkins,
from one of two chartered planes which brought the Wolf Pack
from Reno, Nev., to Tulsa for a game with the University of
A precedent will be set in Oklahoma if Howard or another
player, Alva Tabor, see action in the game.

Tulsa Oklahoma, 1948

...ERSITY OF NEVADA GRID TEAM ARRIVES—Twenty-six members of the University of Nevada football team, accompanied by Coach Joe Sheeketski, arrived from the Mainland by United Airlines plane Thursday morning to play the University of Hawaii Rainbows in the Honolulu Stadium Friday night. The team was greeted by a large crowd of UH officials and students, including Yaocho Greene, UH coed, as the campus "Wolf Girl," and Bill Murray as King Kamehameha. (Advertiser photo.)

UNDECIDED TODAY

Nevada's Use of Negroes May Set Precedent

TULSA, OKLA.—(AP)—Whether a precedent in the University of Tulsa today against the University of Tulsa. Tulsa meets the University of Nevada here Saturday—that of playing Negro football players against Tulsa.

Joe Sheeketski, coach of the undefeated Wolfpack, said still a question today.

Joe Sheeketski, coach of the undefeated Wolfpack, with his squad which includes two Negro backs. He failed to give a definite "yes" or "no" answer when playing the Negroes against Notre Dame.

Sherman Howard and reserve quarterback Alva Tabor.

U. of Nevada 'Wolf Pack' Greeted Here

By DAN McGUIRE
Advertiser Sports Writer

Worried by a lack of practice in the past week and a minimum of information about the University of Hawaii team, Coach Joe Sheeketski and 26 University of Nevada players arrived in Honolulu Thursday morning via United Air Lines for Friday night's game with the Rainbows at the Stadium.

"There's been so much snow in Reno the past week we've been unable to work out," Sheeketski said. "I'm afraid we won't be very sharp against Hawaii. And I don't know about the Rainbows. The scores of their games with Michigan State, Redlands and Texas Mines."

STAN HEATH, the Wolf Pack's All-American quarterback, received special attention from the crowd of UH officials and students who gathered at the airport to welcome the Nevada squad. Dr. Iwao Miyake, acting athletic director at the local institution, and Coach Tommy Kaulukukui were on hand for the greeting.

Nevada Stars May Miss Tilt

RENO, Nov. 21. (UP)—Two of the University of Nevada football stars may be flying to Tulsa today and may have to sit on the bench Saturday when the Wolf Pack meets the University of Tulsa, Coach Joe Sheeketski said today.

Sheeketski said fullback Sherman Howard and Alva Tabor, colored players would not be permitted to make the trip unless Tulsa University officials would give him definite confirmation as to the policy of the school.

Univ. of Nevada, Honolulu, HI 1948

A Glimpse from the Past
Quotes from *Jet* Magazine

Sherman Howard and Marion Motley scored touchdowns as the Cleveland Browns whipped the National League champion Los Angeles Rams, 37-7 in a rough game at Cleveland. Howard scored on a 13 yard pass.

10/9/52, pg. 49

****

The Cleveland Browns...now figure ex-New York Yankee star Sherman Howard in their trend toward more youth and more speed. Coach Paul Brown...inserted Howard into the offensive left halfback slot to give the team more offensive punch.

8/28/52, pg 58

Sherman Howard, Wedding day, 1949

--- CHAPTER 3 ---

PROFESSIONAL FOOTBALL, MARRIAGE AND CHILDREN

My mother, Lillian, was a beautiful woman, raised in a very religious and restrictive home in southern Illinois before moving to Chicago at the age of ten or eleven. Her place of birth was near Cairo, Illinois, where the lower Mississippi River became part of the upper Mississippi River. She was the youngest of four children and her father was a busy pastor in the Church of God in Christ denomination.

Her mother was a homemaker and as a pastor's wife, she was always busy with church activities. My mother exhibited the same qualities as her mother until an addiction to alcohol changed her own personality. I can't help but wonder whether she felt rejected as a child, knowing my grandmother's strict and stoic character. From my teenage years on, my relationship with my mother revealed an emotionally troubled woman. She often demonstrated low self-esteem along with a constant need for encouragement, affection and appreciation. Years later, however, after her struggle with alcohol ended, I witnessed a more independent woman who reached out to help the less fortunate in her Senior Living apartment building.

After much frustration in my own thirty-six years of marriage, I am consciously working on building my self-esteem so that words or actions don't offend or cause me to turn to a substance for comfort. In many ways, my father's background and experiences caused him to develop intolerance for undisciplined individuals. As the family provider, Daddy sometimes had to work two or three jobs for the well-being of his family. As a result, my sisters and I always had plenty of food, many extracurricular activities, and a comfortable place to live. Even after my parents' divorce in 1965, Daddy made all the major family decisions. In fact, we had to get permission from him for just about everything we did outside the house. In whatever he choose to do, Daddy was very thorough, especially in his consistent alimony payments to my mother until her death in 1993.

Their marriage began with a unique challenge because Daddy's training and games during football seasons took him away from home for several months out of the year. It was in December 1949, at the end of his first season with the New York Yanks, that he married my mother in Chicago, Illinois. Nine months later, my oldest sister, Triane, was born. At that time the Yanks were an All American Conference team, but in 1950 they merged with the New York Giants of the NFL. The newly merged NFL Yanks only lasted until 1951, at which time they moved to Texas. Daddy chose not to follow the team and was signed by the Cleveland Browns in 1952.

By March of 1953 my sister, Yvette, was born. I could not help but wonder why my mother stayed in Chicago all that time, so I asked Daddy why my mother did not live with him in Cleveland. Daddy said:

> I wasn't making that kind of money where I could maintain two homes. A lot of guys lived in Cleveland, and that was fine for them. You cannot say I am going to New York and then when I leave there I am coming to Chicago.... No, you better have some place to come back to. We were paid enough money to carry us all year, but you could not maintain two homes with that.

> We were primarily living in hotels so you had to pay more money. It was more expensive. You

did that until you got ready to go to work. I wasn't thinking of football as a lifetime job. It was primarily something you did and you enjoyed the experience and you made some nice contacts. I scouted for seven years after that. That's the only way I maintained three kids.

I asked him how much he made while he was playing professional football in the fifties. Daddy replied:

I made $7,000 a year. That was more than a whole lot of others were making. Some of the others were making $5,000 and some guys were making $3,500. Buddy Young was larger and George Taliaferro, who was an All American from Indiana University and the first black player drafted by the NFL, was larger.

Now you have to remember, most blacks coming into the league were paid way below everybody else. There were not that many blacks anyway, but many whites were at $3,500. The few blacks that came in at that time, after 1949 or '50 did make a little more money, but [some of] those whites who played before that (it was dominated by whites before that), made $3,500.

Some blacks who came in, say with the Giants, made $3,500. Salaries were very low.

Jibri asked his grandfather how close his relationship with Buddy Young was; he was considered one of the fastest black running backs in that era. Daddy replied:

Buddy was born in Chicago and he had a different philosophy about life, period, much different than I did. We went to the same high school, but he was a different type of person. Different values. There was loyalty and close friendship, but back then we had to be close as part of that environment 'cause we were only a few blacks. George Taliaferro was the same way.

In our twenties, we were all sort of establishing ourselves as individuals. Earl Banks, another black teammate, also went to the same high school with me, and we remained close friends in that professional football environment. By being so close in that society, you find that everybody has different personalities. So you accept them for what they are, not the way you want them to be.

Jibri then asked Daddy whether he felt like he had to accept them because they were all trying to break the color barrier. Dad replied:

> Oh yeah. There was no friction because you're able to do what you wanted to do. In terms of cooperating and things like that, that was not necessary because the sport itself dictated your conduct. We were very conscious of not portraying a bad image. Then at the end of the season, I would come back home, and Buddy would come home, as well. While at home, we would see each other occasionally.
>
> Buddy was a star, making $20,000 a year in 1947. That was a lot of money. He'd also get a $10,000 bonus. Buddy had the name recognition and he had a lot of the publicity. I had particular skills that he didn't have; therefore, when you get on the team in pro football, I do not care who you are; you are going to be tested to find out just how good you are. The publicity didn't matter; there were no exceptions, period.

I had more stardom at that time than he did in terms of the teams we were playing on. I was very versatile; for example, I could catch the ball and score points, could run back kicks, could block, and I weighed two-hundred pounds at six-feet tall. Buddy weighed in at one-hundred-sixty-five pounds and was five-feet-four. So that's a big difference in terms of playing. So my skills were evident immediately when we started playing pro football with the Yankees.

Let me put it this way: [if] I hit him, he is going down. If he hit me, I'm not necessarily going down. Now as for Buddy in the skill development, he was fabulous as far as quickness and getting out there in the open. If you break the line of scrimmage, you still have to get further past the line. Buddy was very good at doing that. So that was the difference.

According to Daddy, Buddy did very well for himself:

In 1966, he became the first black administrator hired by the NFL. In fact, his first NFL job was as the assistant to the commissioner. He and the commissioner were close.

Pete Roselle, who was the commissioner at that time, and Buddy had a close friendship. This friendship gave Buddy a powerful tool in making decisions.

Daddy continued:

At the time of his death, Buddy was the Director of Player Relations for the NFL. You could say Buddy died doing what he loved, being involved in football. The NFL bosses had sent him down to Louisiana because one of the players drowned while trying to save some local kids. They sent Buddy down to represent the NFL at his funeral. He went down there, and after the funeral, he had to drive from right outside Monroe, Louisiana, back to Fort Worth, Texas, to catch a plane. On September 5, 1983, in Terrell, Texas, Claude "Buddy" Young, nicknamed the "Bronze Bullet," and one of the shortest men to play NFL football, fell asleep at the wheel and died in a car accident.

The way Daddy described the NFL of the past seemed markedly different from today's more corporate league. He remarked:

Before Buddy died, if someone needed a job, the NFL would create a job for you. Buddy would call up one of the team owners and say, "I've got somebody who needs a job." And they would create a job for you. You did not have to ask about a specific job; they would just create it. You could become the assistant to the assistant. They would make a spot for you.

Now, of course, you had to have the marketable skills. That's the way the network goes. If you know someone in higher places, they'll create a job for you. If I say I have a kicker, or a grandson, the first question they will ask is, "What can he do?" So if he got the job, he got a job representing me. So when he went there, he can't be saying "I'll do this and this and this." No, he'd be representing me. He has to be able to do what he says he can do.

My father, along with Buddy Young, George Taliaferro and Earl Banks, were the black stars of football during the early fifties. They were all frequently mentioned in newspapers and periodicals like *Jet* magazine. My father maintained a close friendship with Earl Banks until his death in 1993, and he and Taliaferro speak frequently on the phone to this day. My father, however, never intended to make a long career of football and faced his next big challenge of marriage and family like he faced everything else in his life, with hope and courage. I asked him what getting married for the first time was like. Daddy replied:

> I got married the first time in 1949 when I was twenty-five. Your mother and I had been dating for a while after I got out of the service, so I decided I would get married. It wasn't any big passionate thing. She was a friend of a friend. In addition, at that time I wanted feminine companionship. I was attracted to her because she was somebody I knew. I was lonely when I came back from the service and I didn't really know anybody in Chicago. Everybody I knew was teenagers. Although they were mostly women, but a three-year age gap is a big difference, from eighteen to twenty-one. Back then, you decided you wanted to get married so you could have kids; however, that was also the beginning of another career for me.

Daddy continued:

I was playing pro football from 1949, when we first got married, to 1954. We moved in 1953 to a bigger place after Yvette [my older sister] was born. At first, we had only one bedroom and Yvette was sleeping on the couch in a baby bed. Then a guy I played softball with told Cliff Davis I needed an apartment. Cliff was managing apartment buildings and he helped me get a bigger apartment for $95 a month, which was unheard of. That was phenomenal, all that room we had down there. I stayed there for ten years with a wife and three girls until I realized your mother and I were just two different people. We were unequally matched.

Daddy's use of the term "unequally matched" reflects my father's biblical perspective on his life. It describes the situation couples have when their beliefs, values, and behaviors conflict with one another.

Daddy continued to reflect on that period of his journey:

I scouted, looking for new players in the NFL for seven years, working on the weekends. After a knee injury, I had stopped playing football and worked for the Chicago Board of Education as a Physical Education teacher. I would send my scouting report in and go to New York once a year. Then they wanted me to go permanent. That meant I would leave the house on Mondays and come back Saturday night[s]. I would go to colleges during the week because you'd have to see what kind of character that player had; then you watch them play during the week. Jerry Rice, who was breaking records in college as a receiver, was on my list of prospective players at the time. There were people who were not on the list, who played well, that I would send in a report on. It was nice: an unlimited expense account, first-class hotels, airplanes—as long as I had a receipt for it, I could do anything I wanted.

Daddy continued:

For me the use of time was my most important factor. But I wanted to teach. Just being around my family, being able to come home at night, was important because I worked three jobs one time: schools, park district at night, and scouting on the weekends for a hundred dollars a week.

> A person told me once that time is your most important element 'cause you can't recapture it. I could have been always away making money, but I wouldn't have been home. But if one of my kids called asking me to pick them up, I could do that.

When my sister and I were young girls, we had a respectful and loving relationship with our father. My mother, Lillian, was a stay-at-home mom who always made sure we had three square meals, clean clothes, and the straightest hair. When afros became fashionable, Momma put the pressing comb away and watched our hair and rebellions increase. When Daddy was home, he sat and manipulated a large reel-to-reel tape player, and his three girls danced and enjoyed the best of old-time jazz music for hours. He also introduced us to various operas, classical music, and movie soundtracks like *West Side Story, South Pacific,* and *Porgy and Bess.* My love for all kinds of music is rooted in those happy times. When he told me how the "Victrola," the premier record player, was enjoyed daily in their house, I totally understood and appreciated his enjoyment of music.

Even after my parents divorced, my sisters and I spent many hours in that same living room listening to the same movie soundtracks, but we added more "45" records from Motown and pretended to be the Supremes or some other famous R&B group. Using our living room as the stage, we were the Karaoke queens of our time before Karaoke became popular.

My two sisters and I grew up in a middle-class neighborhood on the south side of Chicago. The people in our apartment building were professional people such as nurses, teachers, and secretaries. We lived in a spacious three-bedroom apartment located near a low-income, predominately black neighborhood. Just a few blocks to the southeast, however, was the upper-middle class neighborhood of Hyde Park, the same neighborhood where President Obama and his family reside when they are not at the White House.

This integrated neighborhood included many people and families associated with the University of Chicago, along with famous residents such as Heavyweight Champion Muhammad Ali; the Honorable Elijah Muhammad, leader of the Black Muslims; Oscar Brown, Jr. and many more. Some of the best elementary and high schools in the city of Chicago were located in Hyde Park, and we were fortunate to attend school, ride bikes, and play with friends in this safe neighborhood.

In 1968, while I was in the seventh grade, my French class planned and raised enough money to send us to Paris, France, for two weeks. That unusual experience, along with having friends from all races and socio-economic backgrounds, gave me a mostly positive childhood experience without racial hatred. Due to my very fair skin, most of the unkind treatment I experienced growing up was not from whites but from my dark-skinned classmates, who called me "Casper," referring to the cartooned ghost.

To some degree, that attitude among blacks existed throughout my youth. Yes, skin-color prejudices existed even in the black community, a place filled with people of various shades of color. My childhood experiences taught me an important lesson about recognizing and honoring the soul within a person, and gave me an appreciation for the variety of colors we find in humanity. My family had the full range of skin colors, making us a reflective microcosm of the earth's population.

My father made sure we were active in all kinds of sports. We were on the swim team at the Hyde Park YMCA and participated in gymnastics and indoor roller-skating. We also went to camp every summer and frequently rode our bikes to nearby Lake Michigan on hot summer days.

My oldest sister, Triane, became a teacher in the Chicago public schools just like my father. Ironically, Triane had the most conflicts with Daddy over boyfriends, academics, and social life. Her death in 2005 made us all reflect on the many tribulations she went through in school and as a single parent.

My sisters and I occasionally heard my mother hint that Daddy had been involved in some sort of extramarital affair while playing with the Cleveland Browns away from home, but I always pushed that to the back of my mind. While it seemed very important to my mother, it seemed of little consequence to her children.

Several months ago I got the courage to ask my father about the alleged incident and his response was typical of Sherman Howard: no excuses, just the facts. He said, "I was away from home many months, and being a professional athlete, there were many women who saw an opportunity to exercise their seductive nature." True to his nature, my father was very conscious of the energy being directed toward him and continued with, "It wasn't always the man making the first move." So, it is what it is, or in this context, what it was.

From the beginning of his marriage in 1949, my father was away in New York and later Cleveland in 1952, while my mother remained behind in Chicago. In the meantime, she met new friends and developed her own social life, which eventually led to her alcohol addiction. Her heavy social drinking started when I was very young; consequently, I have many sad memories of her as an alcoholic and very few memories of the happy times we had with her.

Some of my happier memories, however, included trips to my maternal grandparents' home during the summer, when my Uncle Mark would drive my mother and us three girls in his Cadillac, several hundred miles to visit southern Illinois. Uncle Mark was like a second father to us. He married my mother's sister, Lynette, and after Aunt Lynette died in the sixties we still spent many happy fun-filled days with Uncle Mark. He owned a barber shop and every Saturday we spent the day doing chores he assigned us, like sweeping up the hair and adding the receipts. In the afternoons, we looked forward to cheeseburgers, fries, and cokes at McDonalds. Daddy couldn't afford to take summers off, so we were blessed to have an uncle who took us on a vacation every summer.

When discussing my mother, Daddy said:

> Your mother didn't work. One of the things your mother and I used to argue about was that she had the skills and was a registered beautician;

however, she would only do her friend Norma's hair, Elizabeth's hair, and your Aunt Lynette's. She had a room in the back of the apartment and I bought her a dryer. All she had to do was set up the business right in the house and do like Ruby and all of them did, bring [her] customers in.

Daddy continued:

Your mother had a drinking problem, as you know. If the problem had happened right now, I would say that I would deal with it; however, when I was young, at that stage twenty or thirty, I said, "No, I must leave." I never thought about whether she had to work because I took care of the rent, [and] gave her money for you[r] all's food, clothes, and whatever was needed.

When you are unequally yoked, the awareness of your differences becomes obvious, especially as you get older. You go home but you really don't want to go home. And so that causes changes. The worst thing in the world is to hate to go home. You've got to provide an environment that is comfortable and free of conflict and tension. As you know, we divorced in 1963.

It is sadly ironic that my mother probably never realized my father had experienced the same addictive behavior with his mother and her friends as he was now experiencing with his wife and her friends. By the time I was in the fifth grade at Reavis Elementary School, my father and mother had divorced, but true to his character, he continued to adequately provide for us. We visited with him regularly and he made sure we knew he loved us as much as he always had. Even today, as in the past, my sister and I greet my father and say goodbye with a kiss on the lips and a hug.

In his book, *The Measure of a Man*, actor Sidney Poitier writes that the most important lesson he learned from his father was that a man is measured by "how well he provides for his children." The fact that my father was an outstanding provider strongly influenced me to marry a man of that same character, and I've been married to that man for thirty-two years. Over the years, as I've struggled to understand my husband and myself, I grew in patience and love, proving that finding a provider was only a first step in my quest to achieve a harmonious relationship.

I find it interesting that Sidney Poitier and my father, both of the same generation, raised their girls in big cities (New York and Chicago), that they were pioneers in their respective endeavors, and that they came from very humble beginnings. While their journeys were similar, the location of my father's birth and a strong maternal influence informed his perspective on life.

I asked my dad why he decided to marry again. He replied:

> Now I was living with Mr. Ferguson, a good friend of mine. Mr. Ferguson and I lived together and I took care of everything. I'd tell women in a minute that I had four daughters and two wives just to throw them off. They would start leaving me alone after that. I stayed with Mr. Ferguson four years, which was when I started dating Lisa. She and I lived together, then Lisa said, "Let's get married and I'll help you with the kids."

I was thirteen when my father married his second wife. My sisters and I adjusted very well to our new stepmother. Many times, however, I felt guilty leaving my mother at home to share time with my father and his new wife.

While my mother continued to drown her sorrows in alcohol, my stepmother, who was well educated in Home Economics, was teaching me how to sew and cook. To this day, she and I stay in touch and I greatly appreciate the seeds of wisdom and knowledge she planted during my teen years and beyond.

Lisa's passion was, and is, playing Bridge. Many times I helped her set up two or more tables for her parties with friends and she traveled a lot to participate in Bridge tournaments. She was not the athletic type, so it didn't really surprise me when that marriage ended after six years.

I was curious to know what my father thought of Lisa, so I asked him. Daddy replied:

> We were married from 1968 to 1974. She was independent, had her own money, but different interests than I did. I noticed the differences in the beginning and most people would tolerate [them], but after a while, I got to the point where her independence influenced my decision to move on. She was able to buy a $40,000 condominium; I didn't have to worry about her being destitute. She could always leave whenever

she got ready, so it wasn't that bad of a thing.

Now my [third] wife and I, we have a relationship; we're equally yoked. I tell her all the time I'd rather be her friend than her husband. She treats her friends well. I mean, you don't have to worry about her. She'll treat you all better than she treats me. That's the way she is.

Then I asked him whether he had more respect than deep love for his second wife.

Oh, yeah. Right. Everybody, like the guy says, you gonna treat with respect; however, as far as my relationship with my wife, the relationship is different from just being married. You know, you talk. She and I would just talk even before we got married. We would just sit down and talk. Openness. Some people are open with you. They will tell you things. Anybody will tell you about their joys as well as their sorrows. That's a different person or relationship. She would tell me about the other guys she dated and share her true feelings about them. Most people aren't going to tell you that. They just put on a big show as if they're so smart, but she's not like that. That's the way our relationship has been.

Now, being husband and wife is altogether different. I don't care how you look at it. Friends and all like that, fine. But when you get married, it's a different story. You go along a while, and then they always say everything is all right until you say something they don't like. And that's when you find out that ego problem. But when you just have a friendship you don't worry about anybody's ego.

So you get to the stage now, at my age of eighty-five, where you realize all that's fine, but your number one priority is God. Once you get that, everything you do is serving God; then you don't have to worry about all that. In the first and second marriages I didn't have that perspective. I've grown into that. I'll wash dishes and that's serving God. I don't have to worry about all that other stuff. Whatever you want me to do, if you want me to go to the store, it's God and me.

About ten years ago my perspective changed. I realized things happen and you don't pay attention to circumstances; you just watch and see what God is trying to tell you. When you think like that, you don't worry about the circumstances. You just have to go through your circumstances; that's all, and you know God's with you. You live a good life. I'm eighty-five and I've been blessed. Very blessed.

These girls today get out into the world and get scarred by the world. Between fifteen and eighteen you're not really touched by the world. But once you get out here and get scarred and knocked around by the world, you change. You change your whole philosophy. Many of these women today are just out for what they can get.

By the time I came along in March 1955, my father was one year into a teaching career that would last another thirty-one years. He started as a Physical Education teacher at a Chicago elementary school, and five years later, he moved to Harlan High School, on the south side of Chicago, where he would work for another twenty-seven years as a Physical Education teacher, football coach, and Athletic Director.

He was born to be a teacher; he had a passion for it. His three girls were the recipients of many lectures. We frequently heard teachings like:

> There are three types of children. The first type you only have to tell them once to do something and they do it. The second type you have to tell them twice before they do what you say, and the third type you have to hit them over the head before they move.

My sister, Yvette, still remembers Daddy's favorite answer to many situations: "It's all about how you were raised." I was the youngest of three girls and my other sisters, Yvette and Triane, were two and five years older, respectively. Yvette and I shared the same bedroom, while Triane had her own room up the hall next to our parents' room. Yvette and I, both Pisces, had similar personalities and Triane, the Libra, often demonstrated her uniqueness with behavior that gave her the attention she learned to love as the firstborn. Triane would often call me "Miss goody two shoes," which highlighted our different natures, especially when I criticized her messy room. Another sibling, Sherwin, wasn't born until 1983, as a result of marriage to my father's third wife. So my sisters and I had to watch Daddy raise another child in his retirement years, while we struggled with our own families.

*New York Yanks Team in 1950, Sherman Howard,
last row, 4th from right*

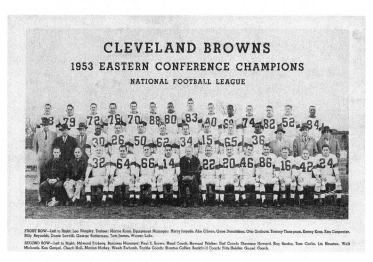

*Sherman Howard (2nd row, 4th from left) with
Cleveland Browns in 1953*

Sherman Howard, Halfback, Cleveland Browns, 1952-53

1949 New York Yankees. Sherman Howard, Back Row, 1st on left

Buddy Young, George Ratterman, George Taliferro
and Sherman Howard (46)

Sherman Howard with teammate, Buddy Young (80), 1949

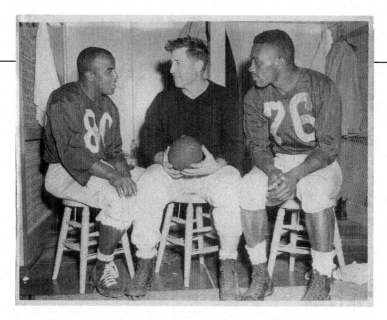

Buddy Young, Red Strader, and Sherman Howard, 1949

****

A Glimpse from the Past
Quote from *Jet* Magazine

Buddy Young scored once on a pass and Sherman Howard took passes of 50 &35 yards to set up two more scores as the surprising New York Yankees tied the Detroit Lions 24-All.

11/1/1951, pg. 53

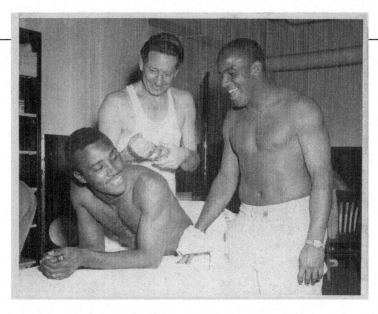

Sherman, Gus Mauch, and Buddy Young

****

A Glimpse from the Past
Quote from *Jet* Magazine

At Green Bay Wisconsin backs Sherman Howard and Buddy Young scored key tallies as the New York Yankees won their first game of the season a 31 to 28 victory over the Green Bay Packers.

12/13/51, p. 50

Red Rooster Café, New York, Nov, 1950
(Celebrities like Sidney Poiter frequented)
(L to R) Sherman Howard (NY Yanks Football), George
Talifero (NY Yanks), Monty Irvin (NY Giants Baseball),
Buddy Young (NY Yanks), Larry Dobey (Cleveland Indians
Baseball, 1st Black player in the American League)

NY GIANTS, 1954, Includes Hall of Famers: Roosevelt Brown, Frank Gifford, Vince Lombardi, Tom Landry and Charlie Conerly. Sherman pictured in the second row, second from the left.

Sherman and his 1st wife, Lillian (my mother)

Sherman Howard at Harlan High School coaching
his young football player.

CHAPTER 4

COACH AND TEACHER

My father taught Health and Physical Education for twenty-six years, from 1959 to 1985, at Harlan High School in Chicago, Illinois, where he held the positions of Athletic Director and football coach. During those years, he invested his time and energy into the lives of thousands of Chicago youths. It was a long-time goal and his heart's desire. I can recall many days we spent with him at his school on "Teacher's Day," in the swimming pool and just tagging along with him as he prepared and planned his lessons.

In 2009, my father and other individuals were inducted into Harlan's honorable listing at a Hall of Fame banquet. As my sister and I entered the hotel for that event we ran into one of my father's former students. After polite introductions, this tall, slightly graying, white guy could not say enough about the influence "Coach Howard" had on his life. He told us the only reason he had come that evening was to honor my dad. Every time I've had a chance to meet one of my father's former students, I've heard the same type of praise and adoration. Obviously, my father's love and dedication to his students paid off, and after many years they continue to show their appreciation.

I asked him what he enjoyed most about his career at Harlan. He replied:

Oh, I had kids who would listen. They'd do what I told them and were very devoted to teachers. They had disciplined kids then. Parents would help you with their kids. I was just talking to one of my former students. All of them did well because they would listen to what you told them. You didn't have to give them solutions but just give them ideas to think about.

Think about it. We have ten judges on the bench now who were former Harlan students. One boy went to the Naval Academy and one is a U.S. Attorney. I go to his house in Hyde Park. Moreover, one guy is a very, very famous artist who teaches school at the Baltimore Art

Academy. Another student is a nuclear physicist who teaches school at University of Texas. Mark Washington played for the Dallas Cowboys, as a cornerback, for ten seasons, and that included five Super Bowls.

And who else? Well, Dennis Rifkin, he graduated from the Naval Academy. So I had a lot of kids who did real, real well. One guy, Bill Campbell, he's been on ABC now for a good thirty years. And one of the other boys, he's a cameraman for CBS. So all of those students did well. That was the type of students we had at that time. They would take the advice of the teachers and explore whatever areas they sent them.

I used to send a lot of kids to college and they came out doing well. One boy now, he does the Martin Luther King "I have a dream" speech every year. He's also a good actor and he's been in several of the black ensemble programs. He was my quarterback. One kid has a very good program out in Las Vegas. So all those kids did well, I think primarily because they listened. They would take your advice and try to utilize whatever information you gave them.

The problem now is they don't take the wisdom of the older generations. They don't believe you know what you're talking about. Your brother was like that for years. He didn't have any reinforcement from other people he met.

At this point in the interview, Daddy brought up a sermon he recently heard about King David that reinforced what it means to be a good listener. When King David ordered Bathsheba's husband to be conveniently killed on the battlefield, Nathan, the prophet, confronted him about his sinful deeds and David repented. This reinforced Daddy's perspective that "Everybody needs a Nathan around them to let them know when they're doing wrong."

Continuing the interview, I asked him how he viewed the teachers at Harlan. He replied:

Very dedicated. All of them. All of them were dedicated. Their first priority was the student. They always ask teachers when they come in to teaching, "Why do you want to teach?" If you don't love kids, you shouldn't be teaching. Those teachers loved kids. All the students said that. They knew that the teachers loved them.

Now most teachers today, they think primarily it's a job. The students are not their number-one priority. You know there's a criteria used when you come in to teaching. There are people who come in to serve themselves and then they serve the school and then they serve God.

It should be just the opposite. You come in to serve God. That's number one. Then you come in to serve the student. Then you come in to serve yourself. But it's just the opposite now 'cause you must come in as if you're serving God when teaching, not yourself. If you come in with that attitude, you're going to be successful. And students recognize that.

That's one thing I tell folks—when I was a student, I recognized a good teacher. I knew who loved the kids and I knew who didn't. We didn't have any teachers when I was coming up who didn't love kids. I can't think of one teacher I thought didn't love kids. Even the hardest ones, we knew they cared about us, [even] one teacher, who everybody thought was so mean and so hard.

But when my mother died that teacher gave me fifty dollars. Do you know what fifty dollars was in 1938? Ooooh that was a lot of money. And teachers weren't making but about a thousand dollars a year or something like that. She gave me fifty dollars to help with my mother's funeral 'cause she didn't have insurance.

Blacks in those days didn't have insurance. You know, some folks had a fifty cent a week burial insurance; however, many folks couldn't afford that fifty cent a week. It was the black insurance companies that started that type of policy. Fifty cent a week, and the insurance men would collect from the people. I knew some guys who were agents. They would write down that you paid your fifty cent. And then they would go around and collect from the people. That paid for your burial and that's all. Burial cost two hundred fifty dollars at that time. That was a lot of money, but that included everything. And the city would give you so much of that.

Now most people were on welfare. We were on welfare. My mother and my aunt were on welfare.

All of them. That's the way it was.

When I asked my father whether it was hard for him to leave Harlan when he decided to retire, his response was, "No, I was always taught you would know when to retire, 'cause when you hate to go to work it's time for you to retire."

"So why did you hate to go to work?" I asked.

> Well, I was getting old. I was in my sixties and I would stand on my feet all the time teaching. In addition, coaching, too, you're on your feet for three hours. I got to the point where my legs got tired and I had to come in and take a little rest.

> Before, when I was younger, I could stand three or four hours at a time just coaching and then do something else afterward. Then I was working two jobs and going to school. I had the energy, and then all of a sudden you realize your body is saying, "Time to retire." A person told me a long time ago, "You don't have to worry about retiring. You'll know when. Your body will tell you when."

Then, also, I began to get kids where I had to change my personality to deal with them. And anytime you have to change your personality to deal with folks, it's time to leave.

What do you mean by "change your personality to deal with the kids?" I asked.

I had certain rules. You do this and you do that. And administrators said, "Well, they're not going to do that."

So I told them, "Well I'm going to have a lot of failures because that's my rule." You know, you come to gym you take a shower after you get through with your activities. If you want a good grade, that's what you have to do; you take a shower. Good students in Physical Ed take showers. Otherwise you're a C student. Now you can come every day, but if you don't shower, uh uh, you're not a B or an A student.

"Oh no can't do that! What? Just coming to gym?" No, no, you're not a good student then; you're not a good Health and Physical Education student. All you're doing is just making an appearance.

You've got to come dressed and prepared. Guys would come in with their pants on and they didn't want to undress or they didn't want to take their shoes off and play in their socks. Uh, Uh. They did not want to wear a supporter. "No, no you can't do that. These are the rules now"; therefore, I had more and more students coming who were not going to abide by the rules, so I had more and more failures because that's my criteria, or you're going to fail. So in order for you to pass gym that's what you had to do.

Now I said I had to change my personality in order to be successful in this area. So rather than change my personality I thought it best that I retire.

Another thing is, I didn't get the cooperation of the parents that I once had. See, before, I would be talking to a student and he would open his mouth and his mom or dad would smack him or hit him in the mouth. But now the parent would say, "I can't do nothing with him."

"Well, how do you expect me to do something with him?" So I become the babysitter for the parents, just keeping them. And in order for me to be successful and deal with them, I'd have to change my rules, and I wasn't going to do that. So they're going to have a whole lot of failures as a result.

When I first started teaching, you might find two or three kids that had problems, so I could help them. They didn't have their gym suit so I would get them one. Now, you come in and you only have a few students who do what you tell them to do. So if you have forty students and only three of them are all right, you can't get thirty-seven gym suits for all the kids. And you get in the swimming area they don't want to go swimming. No, that's part of the program; you have to go swimming. At least get in the water. They didn't even want to get in the water. Now you've got another problem. So it was one problem after another.

And then a lot of parents didn't want their kids undressing in front of other kids. No, you can't have that. That's not part of the program. You have many parents now out here at certain high schools, the kids tell them they don't want to undress or shower in front of other guys. Well, I never had that problem before. Guys don't want to take a shower? You're all boys.

I told them when I was in school, everybody swam naked. That's the way you swam 'cause you couldn't take a chance on a guy having a disease and you didn't see it. If they had a swimming suit on, you can't see what's under the swimsuit. Even when you swam at the YMCA you swam naked. You don't want anybody wearing a swimming suit 'cause they may have just taken it out of the garbage and put it on. So in order to ensure hygienic conditions for the pool, you had to come in and take your shower. You got soap all over you and let the teacher see that you took a shower.

Some of my later students would run in there and run into the gym. No, no, no, I have to see you with soap all over you. That's why we would check their number off when I saw they had soap all over them. Then the guy would come in there saying he was clean and I'd say, "No, no, I have to see the soap." You had to wash your hair, too. They had some of them with greasy hair. No, you can't get in the pool like that.

Those were the rules that were set up. I abided by them and then they began to change. The parents don't want them to do this; they can't do that, and the students would refuse. They'd rather fail gym. Well I'm going to fail them. No, I wasn't going to change, um um. And that's what happened to the Phys. Ed. program, period. People began to change and the kids got so they didn't want to do anything. They didn't want to do exercises.

"And now so many young people are overweight," I said.

Uh huh. And they're not learning good health habits. So you don't have health programs any more. We had health once a week and I'd teach them how to keep their body clean. How to keep their bodies in shape. Then they couldn't say they didn't have the information, and there were some kids that got the information and used it. But if you don't get the information you can't use it. So it has gone by the wayside because now you have very few people take Physical Ed. in school. Very few.

"It's like an option now, isn't it?"

"Yeah, that's an option. That's what Michelle Obama is talking about—the obesity of the children."

Our school systems have failed to follow the "rules" of wisdom. Our youth are spending more time in their seats watching computer and television screens and less time in swimming pools or gym classes. The state of Florida where I live has plenty of opportunities for year-round swimming, yet most schools don't even have a swimming pool to even teach kids how to swim. Is it time for our government to put the health of our kids first with more athletic programs?

Unfortunately, most of the people elected to serve in Washington appear to be swimming in pessimism and greed. If we want to see our youth slim down, we'll have to support more programs like the First Lady's "Let's Move" campaign and take the initiative in our own neighborhoods. First Lady Michelle Obama is bringing a much-needed awareness and attention to the childhood obesity problem in America. Plenty of research overwhelmingly supports the truth that obesity is a serious problem. For information on how to solve this problem, see the Appendix.

My sisters and I were very blessed to grow up with an emphasis on athletic activity. We were members of the YMCA at an early age. Our sports activities included swim team, gymnastics, summer camp, roller skating and bicycling. We got distracted from our exercise, however, once we got a new color TV, so one can imagine the distractions kids face looking at their computers, cell phones and tablets all day. But even though times have changed, the rules for health and fitness haven't! It's our responsibility as parents, grandparents, neighbors, friends and relatives to make a difference in the life of every youth that comes across our path. Plant a seed of truth and conviction to assist the renewal of our children's thinking that has been influenced mostly by the media.

A Glimpse from the Past
Quote from *Jet* Magazine

Sherman Howard, ex-New York Yankees and Cleveland Browns' halfback was named football coach at Chicago's new John Marshall Harlan High School.

1/26/61, pg. 64

****

Halfback Sherman Howard's sensational catch of a 56 yard pass on the Redskin's two yard line set up the Cleveland Browns winning touchdown in a 19-15 home field victory.

11/6/52, pg. 29

Sherman and his young son, Sherwin, 1984-85

Sherman on the golf course, 1984-85

CHAPTER 5

RETIREMENT?

On May 27, 1983, my father's third wife, Jeanette, gave birth to Sherman's first and only son. So most of his retirement years have been spent raising this long-awaited gift. My sisters and I have watched with great interest over the years as Sherman Howard took on this new and exciting task. During those early son-raising years, my father managed to take up golf until an old football knee injury caused him to discontinue that activity.

His son, Sherwin, played sports throughout high school, but continuing sports in college became problematic due to academic challenges. As a result, he is now pursuing a career in computers, which we recognize as a more comfortable and fun venture for him. He has given his father a late life challenge to grow, not just in patience (again) but also in assisting his son's development to full maturity. With a young granddaughter (Sherwin's daughter) in the house occasionally, both my father and his wife, also a retired teacher, have been given a new opportunity to teach and guide another generation to success.

As Sherman coaches his only son toward touchdowns of success on the field of life, the reflections continue:

> These days they've got men age forty and fifty trying to get jobs. My son is competing against them. If a man has three or four kids and you're just out here like my son, they'll hire the older man. The best thing my son can do is to have marketable skills so he can go into certain areas. There are always certain jobs available. In his field, computer engineering, they're begging for him—the FBI, everybody.

> However, he admitted he wasn't ready for college. They didn't have anybody in the colleges who could mentor him and show him the way. They don't have those types of guys. When I was going to school you'd have some guy say, "Come here, boy; what you doing?" You'd have a second family. You don't have that in college now. They have guys who are holding those jobs

as student advisors that make sixty or seventy thousand a year, but they don't do anything.

The coach of Louisiana State recruits blacks right out of high school and can do fabulous things. He went and got the best back in the country going to Alabama; he's only eighteen years old. Now he's going to help Alabama win some games. But he already knows he can only expect him to stay there for two years. And that's the way he recruits. It's not because he likes blacks. But those blacks bring in that money and they help them win those games. LSU had ninety-thousand tickets sold.

You watch Mississippi play Tulane and you think it's two black schools playing. One team has eleven blacks. You watch anyone, Arkansas, all of them play. These guys have got those blacks.

In the NBA they have people like Kobe Bryant. They have to get another black just as good as Kobe Bryant who can play against him. So that's how blacks get these jobs. And the salary scale level, $410,000, is for the rookie in the NFL. All you have to do is play two years. Just make the two years, and that's what makes me mad. My son's got the ability. He's as good a kicker as anybody in the league, but you've got to be in shape.

The guy who's coaching down at Notre Dame (one of my wife's former students), his job is to evaluate the kickers. He told my son to come down and let him look at him. Now if he's good enough, he's got four or five schools he can call. He can get on right away. All he has to do is show the coach he can kick the ball.

He didn't get the grades. I understand. A coach might have twenty scholarships. Out of the twenty only ten might play for him and the rest will sit on the bench. Coach Banks at Morgan State would just say, "Send on down whoever you have." He wouldn't question. Like my granddaughter's mother. She saw a good thing with my son, and a lot of girls are like that. And so they don't have any perspective of what life's all about. Nobody to tell them, so they use that philosophy to get what you can when you can however you can. But there's nobody around to tell them differently. And they don't have any depth with God. They're living their own [lives]. They are their own god[s]. In a way, that's what they're doing.

So later on, they'll say, "Why didn't somebody tell me that?"

"But we tried to tell you, but you didn't listen."

That's one of the problems you have now is the young will not take the wisdom of old folks. So that's the difference now: these guys now, you tell them about something, but they don't believe you. Now my son's almost twenty-six and he's learning all this. But I know guys out here, forty and fifty years old, who aren't that smart. Yvette has worked and now retired, but a whole lot of folks won't reach that stage 'cause they made so many mistakes along the way. It's rough. If you can work and reach a stage where you can retire, you can go out in your pajamas and get your check (or have direct deposit).

Now the biggest problem is like mine, trying to help somebody else. I can take care of myself, but the reason God keeps you here is so you can help somebody else. He's not going to let you sit around and live a good life. He's going to put you to work. I'm trying to help my son and his child. That's my job now. It's a job, but it's a different kind of job. It's a choice/judgement I have to make.

Sherman on the golf course, 1985

Sherman with longtime friend, Tom Landry, infamous coach of the Dallas Cowboys.

A Glimpse from the Past
Quotes from *Jet* Magazine

*...Halfback Sherman Howard (25 yard pass)
scored as the Cleveland Browns beat the
Philadelphia Eagles, 49-7.*

11/6/52, pg. 29

****

*Sherman Howard, the Cleveland Browns'
halfback, underwent surgery for a shoulder
separation which he suffered while making a
sensational catch of a pass in the Redskins game.*

11/13/52, pg. 28

Sherman's three girls (L to R) Yvette, Vietta, Triane, 1956

CHAPTER 6

DEATH OF A CHILD

On September 27, 1950, in Chicago, Illinois, my mother gave birth to a girl, Sherman's first child. They named her Triane, after their landlord's daughter. That birth took place on the same day Sherman Howard, a running back with the NFL New York Yankees at the time, scored three touchdowns in New York City in an exhibition game against the Detroit team. That evening, after three successful catches and scores on the football field, an exhausted Sherman was handed a telegram announcing his new offspring.

Triane was my older sister by five years. My birth took place in 1955, after Daddy had retired from the NFL. Fifty-five years after Triane's birth, we attended her funeral on April 18, 2005, in the city where that birth took place. For several months before her death, the whole family listened to and observed a woman in pain, both emotionally and physically, as she struggled to overcome the loss of her own children.

Triane lived with my family and me in Florida for the nine months preceding her death. She was challenged with an aggressive form of breast cancer the entire nine months before she passed away on April 12, 2005, at 3 p.m. It was one of the most challenging and stressful periods of my life as I witnessed the progression of a disease neither she nor I had any control over. She and I had hope that the fasting, prayer, juicing, and healthy diet would stop the growth of the tumors, but near the end of the battle she very calmly showed me the dress she wanted to be buried in.

The most important lesson I learned from that journey with her became the emotions she held on to, which I believe interfered with her ability to heal. Much of my own healing came from the Psalms and Proverbs as well as the book of Ecclesiastes, important sources of wisdom and peace when seeking to understand death. Ecclesiastes in particular speaks often of the heart and appointed times to live and die, but the highest perspective on death can be found in chapter 7:1-2, which are summed up as the day of death is better than the day of birth because the living take it to heart. While my father and I always agree on our understanding of the Scriptures, he always brings a perspective that far surpasses my fifty-eight years on this earth. Triane's life and death were no exceptions.

Triane followed in my father's footsteps and became a teacher, staying in the Chicago public school system for thirty years. She had witnessed the death of two children, one at birth and one at the age of fourteen. I fully realize now that parents who fail to find peace and purpose in their children's deaths can contribute to much sickness and even send those parents to their own graves. While I saw a Divine plan for my sister's entire life, like most parents, to this day, my father expresses what went wrong or what could have been. He speaks a great deal about her life.

Near the end of our 2009 kitchen-table interview, I mentioned his oldest daughter to him and without any hesitation he began reflecting mostly on the many conflicts he experienced with her:

> The one thing about Triane was she just would never listen. You tell Triane what she shouldn't do and that was one of her problems. She was stubborn. I remember one time her boyfriend was takin' her money. I told her don't be messin' around with somebody who's takin' your money. She went down to Lincoln University and was living with another boyfriend. He left her and married somebody else. But Triane wouldn't listen.

Triane had no guidance. And there was never anyone in her life that would sort of give her encouragement to do that. She was always evaluating people by me. You can't do that. Once she left the house, the world [was] different. And most people are like that. You've got a certain environment you're living in and now going into the world. Once you get out into the world, you've got to have additional support to support what you've already learned or else you've got to be strong enough to learn as you go along.

A lot of people aren't that strong to make adjustments. And that's the whole thing about life—you have to be able to make adjustments, which was the first course we took in college. The guy said, "You'll come up against a wall in life; now how are you going to get across it?"

Some guys will say, "Oh the hell with it" and go back. Some will bore a hole through it; some will figure out a way to go around it. Some might vault over it. Some might get four or five people to get on their shoulders and get up. But there's always some adjustments you have to make to get across that wall.

And one thing about it, God will always give you some knowledge of how to get across it. Some kind of way he'll show you how to get across if you are patient. If you are patient and most people are not patient. They just have their idea. That's why I say the frustration in life is based on your ambition. The more ambitious you are, the more frustrated you can become. See, all I ever wanted was a warm house, three meals a day, and maybe a decent job. And I went beyond that 'cause that was my frustration level I was trying to achieve. Now if I want a million dollars, I want to be driving a Lexus or Cadillac all the time, that's going to bring on frustration.

So my job is like David. He asked for simple things and God gave him more. But again you've got to be in that position where you are. If you say, "I just want to serve," well then, you might get that chance. You've got to be ready for when your well runs dry or your brook runs dry. But when your brook runs dry, the people you once thought would help you, the people you once loved and all like that, you've got to be ready for that. When the things you want or the things you want to do no longer hold out, you've got to go and make the change[s] or adjustments.

Whether you want to admit it or not, you're not here to stay. I count my blessings daily. But you might find out there's a lot of people [who] just can't make it in this world 'cause they can't make adjustments. And that's because they don't trust God.

As my sister, Yvette, and I smiled at each other as we listened to Daddy reflect on Triane and beyond, Yvette interrupted and asked whether he believed Triane trusted God, to which I quickly replied:

In the end, totally! More than I could have. Whatever happens, you have to trust your Creator. I think after her daughter died, that was her adjustment period. She had to learn to trust the Creator for understanding. But before that, I don't think it was totally there. After her daughter, Nyaa died, it was Triane's journey of trusting, trusting.

Daddy picked up the conversation with:

Even when Triane lost that first baby, God was giving her a message—"Trust me." When she was down there in college in Missouri she didn't trust God. When she first went to college in

LaCrosse, Wisconsin, if Triane had gotten that degree she would have had a beautiful life. But she didn't pass anything. So she transferred to Lincoln University and got another chance. But she was messing around with her boyfriend and looking for something she wanted.

After her graduation, when she came back home, I tried to tell her to take that exam to be certified with the Chicago Board of Education. She went down there with her dirty gym shoes. They took thirty points off and she still had a seventy-eight, but with thirty points off. But then again, to show you how the Lord works, that was His will. Someone said, "If you had told me that was your daughter, I would have passed her." But it wasn't to be that way. She'd get a job and was working two jobs, making good money, and she still wasn't satisfied.

There was silence at the table for a few seconds. As I thought about my sister's death, I saw her Divine assignment like never before. She taught us to observe the adjustments or lack thereof: "If you don't make the adjustments, this is what happens." I thought of her name, Tri-ane, as having the number three in it, which can mean Divine perfection and completion in the Bible.

And at the end of her life there were threes everywhere: three tumors in her breast, three tumors in her brain, and she took her last three breaths at three o'clock! *Wow! I thought. Her lesson was one of reaping and sowing, the law of the universe.*

Daddy continued:

> Triane had everything going for her; all she had to do was adjust. After she left Drexel when your mom died, she could have made an adjustment then. OK, she wanted to live in Hyde Park, 'cause she came out here but she wanted to live in Hyde Park so there were nice apartments on Hyde Park Boulevard. One bedroom was about five hundred dollars. But she had to go to eight hundred fifty for a two bedroom on the third floor. She was stubborn. But she had to have it the way she wanted; it had to be the way she wanted it.

Once again, there was silence at the table.

My sister, Triane, had developed expensive taste over the years. My family and I invited her to go to Hawaii with us a year after her daughter's death. My sister decided to purchase a first-class ticket on one of our short flights to another island, rather than risk being bumped on a standby ticket, which is what the rest of us were flying on. As I observed her from the back of the plane in her designer-type straw hat, she looked like a million bucks. But when I look at some of the pictures we took on that trip, I have such mixed emotions. On one hand, it was one of the most harmonious vacations we ever took, but as I look into her eyes, it appears as though she was crying deep inside.

While my father has often stated, "I never thought my child would go before me," he does an admirable job of detaching from the loss and grief and instead takes it to heart with personal reflection. My sister, Triane, on the other hand, remained emotionally attached to the loss of her child and leaves behind a powerful lesson about personal unforgiveness, guilt, and grief. She is the legacy I share with others in my work to bring consciousness and healing to this planet. Her suffering motivated me to publish my first book titled, *My Body is Talking to Me*.

While I was reading a passage of *My Utmost For His Highest*, a daily devotional, on March 22, it reminded me of how well my father controls his emotions and responds to life's challenges with a higher perspective. As usual, the author, Oswald Chambers, states this concept in a deeply, thought-provoking manner:

> Much of the distress we experience as Christians comes not as the result of sin, but because we are ignorant of the laws of our own nature. For instance, the only test we should use to determine whether or not to allow a particular emotion to run its course in our lives is to examine what the final outcome of that emotion will be. Think it through to its logical conclusion, and if the outcome is something that God would condemn, put a stop to it immediately.[3]

My father has demonstrated this principle so well in his life that I am quick to call him for guidance and his opinion on events that happen in mine. Most often, his advice to me, which comes in part from the death of those close to him, is "Expect the unexpected." Words from a wise and deeply caring human being.

A good reputation is more valuable than the most expensive perfume. The day one dies is better than the day he is born...sorrow is better than laughter, for sadness has a refinining influence on us. Yes, a wise man thinks much of death, while the fool thinks only of having a good time now.

Ecclesiastes 7:1-4

****

The Living Bible, paraphrased
Tyndale House Publishers, Inc.
Wheaton, IL
Copyright 1971

Buddy Young and Sherman Howard, 1950

CHAPTER 7

FOOTBALL, POLITICS AND CTE

Sports of all kinds continue to be sources of entertainment for my father in his retirement days. He is fully aware that football has become a biiiiggg business. After all, he's been involved in it for sixty years. We can learn a lot today about how time shapes a sport and an athlete by watching the changes the sport goes through. In the late 1940s, when my father played, the average annual salary a professional football player received was $5,000 to $6,000 a year. Today a first-year player receives nearly $400,000. I asked my father how he sees football today. He said:

> Now they have a scale and a rookie football player makes close to $300,000 with no experience. If they have one year I think they make $400,000. It's way up there.

Then I asked him whether he believed a lot of men were playing more for the wealth and fame than for the love of the game.

Certainly, certainly. It's a job, not a recreation anymore. That's your livelihood. It's how you make your money. Before, a lot of guys just loved playing football and they got less money but they got paid something for playing. Now it's a profession just like a doctor or lawyer. It's just how you make your money.

I also asked him how he would compare the politics of early football to those of football today.

The politics of football today is money. Make all you can, how you can, wherever you can, under whatever circumstances you can. And try to find all the loopholes you can where you don't have to pay taxes. That's from the agents on through the players and the owners. So it's all a money thing now.

Any time you see any controversy in America, it's about money. All this talk about a "health bill." The health bill is all about money. And certain congressmen get paid to try and stop it. All of them are on the payroll of the health industries, pharmaceuticals, insurance companies, doctors, all of them. If they're not on the payroll, they've got their daughters, their wives and sons, everybody else working for them. And when they get through, retire or get voted out of Congress, they go in as consultants or lobbyists.

I think we can look at former Vice President Cheney as an example of that.

And when the war started, his company got all the contracts. They made $3.6 billion in one year off the Iraq war. It's all about greed; it's all about greed. But the American people know all these little secrets now because it's all over the Internet. I don't know why they try and hide it.

Everybody's got devils and they all think they can get away with something. Even the devil thinks he can get away with something but God sees what he's doing. Remember, the devil's a creature of God. God created him, too, so why does he think he's going to get away with anything?

But he thinks like most people do. A whole lot of folks think they can get away with something without anybody knowing it. But that's man's foolishness. Like the Bible says: "man suffers for lack of knowledge." Most people, when you tell 'em something, they say, "Oh where did you get that from?" And I have to tell 'em, Isaiah 46:1 or some other scripture. I say, "Jesus never argued with anybody. He just said it is written. He would quote it."

Today you don't have to be great. Just be good enough to get on the team. Now they're only going to play about twenty some odd guys. The coach keeps the guys he doesn't have problems with. Some of the players in the NFL now, the coaches have problems with them. The players have bad attitudes. But like the guy says, the guy who takes his place is worse than him.

My sister asked him what he thought the NFL would do about Michael Vick, the player imprisoned for dog fighting.

Somebody's going to get him. They're not going to let that skill go away. Now they got people who kill people, so why would they keep Michael Vick out? He's going to make some money. He's got too many good skills. Too many guys out there are ten times worse than he is. Somebody will pick him up, sure. They're going to try and make it look like he's on probation and all that, but he's going to help some team.

He could help the Chicago Bears. But they don't want to deal with the publicity involved with it. See, the Bears make thirty to forty million a year profit off them. You have to pay your money to the Bears for season tickets by April 1st. Fifty-three thousand season tickets paid for. But the season doesn't start 'til September. So they're getting all that interest on that money. But you have to have your money in by April 1st. That's minimum two-and-a-half percent, and they have all that money they're banking. And all the teams do that.

The reason I gave up my seats is I had to pay $3,000 in order to get the privilege of buying a seat. For the privilege of buying a seat I had to give up $3,000. But there are people standing in line trying to get tickets. Everybody's saying, "Oh we're so mad at them."

"Well, let me have your season ticket."

"Oh no, I'm not going to give those up."

They've got a billion-dollar contract with the TV networks. They get that money before the season even starts. So it's big money.

"So that's how they can afford to pay these players," I said.

Yeah. But see everybody hollers about the players but they don't realize the owners are making big money also. They can't holler about that. Plus, these NFL teams are non-profit organizations. I didn't know that 'til last month. They have a whole lot of things they can do.

They have something called a 501(c)3 corporation, where you get all these privileges. I didn't know all that, but you're supposed to put down when you're negotiating, what your profit and loss is on, who's who, and where you pay your salaries. The NFL hasn't been doing that. That's why you don't know who's who.

But all these other corporations are like that; you can go on the Internet and find out what somebody makes. But the NFL hasn't been doing that and they've been getting by with it all these years. But you're supposed to be able to go to the Internet. All that's supposed to be published about a nonprofit organization: all the salaries, what your profits are, what your losses are, and how you put out.

So now that the negotiations have been going on, they want to cut down the amount of money the players get for salaries. See, before, the players would get 60 percent of revenues for salaries. The team owners want to cut it down. But the percentage the owners are getting is huge. But that's the owner's money, the 40 percent they're getting. The other 60 percent is for salaries among all the players. And that doesn't include TV, parking fees, and the money they make on the side. So they're all making money.

The Bears went from $24 million dollars to $250 million. That's how much the Bears are worth. They were $24 million before franchise; now they're $250 million. Dallas is $1 billion. Falcons are way up there, too.

"So that's how much money they bring in?" I asked.

More than that. That's what we know. They're not going to tell you everything.

Now that's what the new commissioner is bringing out. They don't want to hear it, but he's going to publish it and let the public see what they make. That's what they did with Bank of America and all of them. They start publishing what they're doing and a guy's getting $23 million dollars on a company that's failing. You shouldn't do that in business but that's what they do.

While the business and politics of football can be confusing and complex at times, more recent headlines are making the game a clear issue of the heart and head. This became more obvious to me when I received my regular issue of the *On Wisconsin* magazine in December 2010 from my alma mater in Madison, Wisconsin. The cover featured a picture of neuropathologist, Ann McKee, with the headline **"Head Games...the devastating effects of brain injuries in athletes."** I was surprised to read that professional football players on both offensive and defensive lines "...tend to suffer between nine hundred and fifteen hundred sub-concussive hits to the head each year," which is one of the reasons Ann McKee is studying Chronic Traumatic Encephalopathy (CTE).

One of the most heart-wrenching stories in that magazine was that of Mike Webster, a former Wisconsin Badger, but more popularly known as "Iron Mike" of the Pittsburgh Steelers. Mike played seventeen seasons in the NFL, helped his team win four Super Bowls, and was inducted into the NFL Hall of Fame in 1997. Unfortunately, his position of playing center meant leaning over the football before passing to the quarterback, which "...added up to countless instances of cranial trauma." The article further states that "By the time he retired in 1990, he was hooked on painkillers. By 2002, he was dead." Before his passing he had bouts of amnesia, depression, and dementia and spent periods of time "...living out of his truck or at train stations."

After he died, an autopsy was performed on his brain, and he became the first NFL player to be diagnosed with CTE. His family sued the NFL for disability payments and received a judgment of more than $1 million dollars. Since that time, more families have donated players' brains for CTE research. As of 2010, "Every athlete whose brain Dr. McKee has studied who's played more than ten years of contact sports has been diagnosed with CTE." These findings include sports such as boxing and wrestling, as well, in addition to football.

As of 2011, the average NFL career is shown to be between three-and-a-half and ten years, depending on variables such as first round draft picks or opening day rosters. Career lengths actually haven't changed much since my father's football-playing days.

My father played five years of professional football before a knee injury forced him into retirement. In those five years he remembers experiencing one or two mild concussions, which ended up being a Divine tap on the shoulder (also injured in a game).

That knee injury may have actually saved his brain! How many players ignore the physical signs that they've played long enough, especially those frequently using pain medication? Even though we as a family were spared the heartache that many families have experienced from watching their pro players mentally and physically deteriorate, my father did experience a different health challenge that woke him up in some unexpected ways.

*Your word is a lamp to guide my feet
and a light for my path.*

****

*Psalms 119:105
New Living Translation*

CHAPTER 8

KEEPING THE FAITH

In 1993 my father suffered a heart attack. It was a surprise considering the excellent physical shape he's always been in. His doctors performed bypass surgery and for several weeks after, his wife, children, and friends prayed for a complete recovery. He attributed the cause mostly to the many years on a steak and potatoes diet as an athlete. My holistic perception looked more at the built-up stresses in his life and his decision to shovel snow on the day the attack occurred. Thankfully, however, twenty-one years after that major health challenge, I was able to ask him how he reflects on that event. Longevity spoke:

> That slowed me down, but it's the circumstances that let me know God says this and God says that. So you go through changes. Now the tragedy about it is if you go through certain things and don't think about what God is trying to tell you, then you're not paying attention.

I think about 9-11, but they've got people dying every day. Innocent people. You talk about three thousand dying? I was reading the book of Chronicles, and Judah wanted to punish Ephraim on how they treated that woman they raped and murdered down there. God wouldn't let them do it the first two times and eighty-eight thousand people got lost in that fight. Then God finally decided, "OK, I'm going to let you kill them all." And that's why the tribe of Ephraim got destroyed.

My son spoke up at this point and said, "Oh yeah, that was the daily reading on my iPod."

But they say, "Oh we lost three thousand men." Three thousand? That's all? If you read the Bible and see how, five, six, fifteen, or twenty thousand people died in one day. Innocent people in the wilderness. Kids and everybody died coming through the wilderness.

I spoke up and said, "They weren't innocent, but more in the Divine order of reaping and sowing."

Yeah, yeah, right. My former student's wife was killed in 9-11. The way it was, they went down to see their daughter play soccer for North Carolina's team. The wife had to go to New York for something. She was on that plane that went down. The husband came home because he had some work to do, or else he would have been on that plane. They have a lot of stories like that. People got on that plane. They stopped the Pentagon tragedy. But you can't tell people that, 'cause they won't believe you. They think they are master[s] of their fate. Captain[s] of their souls.

And that's what the guy on the news thinks. They let you know every day they're supposed to run everything. They're in charge. My wife always asks me, "Why do you listen to them." I just want to see how ignorant some people are. Yeah, I listen to them because the first thing I ask is, "Who's your authority?"

My son interjected, "But on the news, some of them consider themselves conservative Christians."

Well, this one guy made a statement and I don't think he realized what he was saying: "I believe in torture to save America and I'm a Christian."

He didn't realize what he was saying. Yeah, I believe in anything that would save American lives. Well, what about two-hundred-fifty years of slavery? Did that save American lives? Women not being able to vote 'til 1924? Did that save American lives? All the tragedies, like people getting lynched. Did that save American lives? The question is, "Who's your authority?"

I couldn't help but think about the abortion issue. The man who killed that abortion doctor considered himself a Christian. Randall Terry and all of Operation Rescue consider themselves Christians. And all the people in church with the abortion doctor are Christians. So many Christians are confused.

Christians take an issue they feel is most important, and they decide this is wrong. Like with the gay and lesbian issue. The Bible says no. Now you may want to do it, but I'm not going to say yes to it. But at the same time you're going to have to suffer for your own sins. But I'm not going to OK it and say, "Yeah that's fine."

No, uh uh, I can't be that liberal. I can't say you should do abortions, fornication, and adultery.

I don't see everybody saying "OK come out of the closet all you adulterers; all you fornicators come out of the closet." I don't see anybody saying, "OK do that." So why should you all of a sudden say all lesbians should come out of the closet?

You're sinning. It's just that simple. It's a sin. Now, I didn't say I'm perfect, but I'm not going to come out and tell everybody, "Give an OK for my sinning." But that's what they're saying: OK to my sinning. Oh no, you can't do that.

Well, these are the last days.

But this is the argument: leave man to his own decisions. You mess up the world like they are doing now. You're not that smart. Seek ye first the Kingdom; lean not on your understanding. You get all these blessings if you just follow the wisdom of the Bible, but again you don't have enough people saying that. So what's the Bible say? Man suffers because of lack of knowledge. We perish for lack of knowledge. Suffer and then perish.

Then my sister, Yvette asked, "So what's the greatest spiritual lesson you've learned?"

> Trust God. In All Things! Trust God. Trust God. For every opinion there's an opposite opinion. And nobody's proven that your opinion is right or his opinion is right. The only one that proves your opinion is right is God. That's all you do is trust God. That's my biggest consolation. Trust God. I used to worry about everything; no, just trust God. That's all you can do. That's what Solomon said. Trust God. Ecclesiastes, that's the last verse in that book. The last verse, trust God. Keep his commandments and trust God. That's all you can do 'cause when it's all said and done, you can't do nothing about it. Ain't nothing you can do about it.

"Any last words for your children and grandchildren?" she asked.

> "Trust God. All the guys I know having problems now, they didn't do that. Lean not on your own understanding."

Yvette nodded and said, "I shall remember that. The one

thing I remember that you always said is, 'It's all about how you were raised.' You always used to say that."

Both my sister and I nodded and said, "Amen, Amen!"

Then Yvette asked, "You and Thomas, your long-time friend and teammate, are pretty close, but does he have that faith?"

"If you push him through it, he'll admit it. But he's not open. He thinks he can change things by his own initiative."

"Without God's help?" Yvette replied.

Well, while he's doing it, unless somebody mentions it to him. But while he's doing it, he thinks he's doing it. I always tell him about the guy drowning and he prayed, "Please, Lord, help me; help me." And the log comes along and he says, "Sorry, Lord, I don't need you[r] help." Because he believes the log came along without God's help. And so a lot of people do that. They'll make things and they think they did it.

Like this thing in Iran. That's God's work. I was telling folks when Obama was running, "If God wants him to win, he will win." Now he's doing you a favor, not you doing him a favor 'cause I don't think anybody else could have handled what's going on now better than Obama. That's what Michelle said. Michelle said, "You all are blessed to have my husband as President." She said, "He's a blessing to this country. And we don't know how lucky we are." They can't understand that.

Father Hesburgh (at Notre Dame) said after Obama's speech, he'd never seen a man give a speech that long without notes or prompts. He was fascinated by it. He did not use any prompts or nothing for a whole hour. Even if he memorized it, most people can't memorize speeches. That's God's blessing.

I've seen guys memorize a speech for twenty minutes, but a whole hour? That's unheard of. And he's not stuttering or anything. I'm just pleased to see there is such a person that exists like that. I just like to hear him talk, to watch how he answers questions and how he does things.

The best thing I tell anybody to do is listen to Obama and learn. You just listen and learn. Don't try and evaluate him and things like that. Just listen and learn. When you read the Bible, you can't be judging and all like that. You read and learn! You know, 'cause everything they say they don't stop and say, "No here's the answer right here."

God always gives you alternatives. He doesn't criticize you. But he gives you alternatives: "What if you did it this way? Try and see if this works. See if this would be better for you than that way."

You tell folks that over and over again. But the hardest part about all that is patience. You got to have patience. Be still and have patience. And everybody I know who has ever had troubles is not patient. And while you are doing what you're supposed to be doing. Just like the guy was saying about chasing butterflies. You chase butterflies; you're not going to catch any butterflies. But if you just go about your business and do what you know, a butterfly will come and land right on your shoulder.

CHICAGO VARSITY CLUB, 1970's: First Row, R to L: Sherman J. Howard, Ozzie Simmons, (All American Half Back, Iowa State, 1930) Wilson Frost, (3rd Ward Alderman, Chicago) Dr. Ziegler, Dentist. Second Row, R to L: Edward Christian, Jesse Owens (Olympic Gold Medalist), Wesley Ward (Chicago Park Supervisor), Ink Williams, (All American Football at Brown University, 1920)

CHAPTER 9

A HEAD ABOVE THE REST: A TIME TO CELEBRATE

When Obama took the oath to become President, my father, along with several million others, was moved to tears. Many never thought they would see the day when a man of color would take that oath. Knowing my father's history, I believe those tears brought healing to the many wounds from the hatred others directed to him over the years. A multiracial, multicultural people elected Obama to the highest office in America based on his character more than his color. The younger generation is becoming color-blind and starting a cycle of optimism, humanism and an expansion of the inner light to overcome our dark past.

In his State of the Union speech on January 27, 2010, President Barack Obama highlighted this truth when he said:

The only reason we are here is because generations of Americans were unafraid to do what was hard, to do what was needed even when success was uncertain, to do what it took to keep the dream of this nation alive for their children and grandchildren.

Those words can be interpreted in many ways. The words "courage" and "fearless" can also be used to refer to the pioneers who risked their lives to do what was righteous. The courage men like my father displayed, to do "what was needed" has paved the way for more positive and healthy relationships between races. Sherman Howard didn't just make an impact on racism, but maybe, more importantly, he helped influence thousands of inner-city youth, both black and white, to succeed.

In the movie "Men of Honor" actor Cuba Gooding, Jr. who won an Academy Award for his role, does a remarkable job of displaying the emotional side of the racial prejudice and hatred black men had to endure. It's a moving portrayal of the first black Navy diver, Carl Brashear, who advanced to the top of his field even after one of his legs was amputated below the knee.

This movie reminds us of the determination and strength of character that kept these men persevering. They may not have perfect personal relationships (Brashear was married and divorced three times), but they succeeded in a mission far greater than most of us could ever imagine. Brashear's son states on a YouTube video that his father "...loved himself and loved people." It's a beautiful statement about the reality of loving oneself first before we can truly love others. It also says a lot about loving the Creator and trusting the circumstances to bring about an ultimate good.

My two sons grew up in mostly white neighborhoods and had friends of all races. Today, race is not an issue for them, and they truly judge character above all else.

So who are the pioneers of today? Recently, while waiting for a friend to finish her shopping at a local grocery store, I picked up a magazine. There was an interesting article written by a man living in the U.S. who happened to be of European descent and was married to a Haitian woman. He used the term "Obama generation" to describe the biracial children of today and elaborated on the challenges he faces as the parent of a biracial child. These children appear to be growing in numbers and are visual reminders of our need to let go of racial labels. Today, with such sophisticated DNA analysis, a blue-eyed blonde could have black ancestors, but that just makes him or her more "human." Death comes to all of us, no matter what the color of our skin is, and the final judge is a spirit of love. How are we measuring up in our love game?

A song by India Irie gives us a clear and simple perspective: "Spirit knows no color; either you're a hater or a lover." And, as the universe moves in cycles, we will reap the consequences of hate or love. So are we going to play the race game or the human game? We can learn much from the fearless, fully prepared men and women who were driven by a holy wind of change. Whether in a business suit, a football uniform, a diver's suit, or a baseball uniform, it's absolutely essential that we love the human faces of different colors if we are to stop the cycle of hate and prejudice. As Michael Jackson sang, "I'm starting with the man in the mirror..."

These words from the book, *My Utmost For His Highest* by Oswald Chambers seem to sum up the mission that was before Sherman Howard and other pioneers like him: "Then there is the call to spiritual perseverance. A call not to hang on and do nothing, but to work deliberately, knowing with certainty that God will never be defeated.... Continue to persevere spiritually."[5] As we persevere in the love of our Creator, we know that "perfect love cast out all fear." We are guaranteed success in whatever mission we choose if we keep the higher perspective.

So who is the Obama generation? A limited perspective says it is composed of biracial offspring. A higher perspective suggests this generation has <u>all</u> the positive characteristics that our current President has demonstrated from the time he stepped on the scene until now. Members of this generation are fearless, intelligent, family oriented, concerned for the needs of others, and possesses a love for their multicultural heritage demonstrated toward themselves first and all humans second. This generation has a responsibility not only to remember our history with its cycles of hatred and pain, but to recognize or discern the negative energy in our society that still exists and choose to infuse love into the environment. As each of us becomes fully conscious of the unhealthy relationships in our society, whether at home or the workplace, we have an opportunity to shine the light of love, compassion, and understanding in that environment. One light at a time bringing healing and restoration to negative situations can make a difference in this war-torn earth.

As we observe the confusion and debates in Washington, there seems to be a severe lack of wisdom and discernment. Instead of light filtering out from our government, there seems to be mostly darkness and fear. My father and I have frequent conversations about the issues of our day and the various opinions expressed. Even with thirty years between us, we agree that the Creator's perspective is the most important. My father watches Christian TV throughout his day, so naturally he has opinions about the many sermons he hears. He recently made the comment, "I scan the religious channels now, and it's a lot of theatrics. Everybody goes for the show," which is one of the reasons I stopped watching Christian TV. I think we are both looking for spiritual meaning in every circumstance.

It appears that too many people in Washington don't have a spiritual clue. If they did, there would be a collective effort to help Obama succeed so that children of color might be motivated to dedicate their lives to making a difference in the world. Instead, we are witnessing what appears to be the same cycle of prejudice and hatred that could cause more discouragement and pain than in years past. The younger generation must recognize the need to stop the cycle of hate, ignorance, and pain, creating a wave of opportunity to bring healing to our earth.

My father endured and observed much physical and mental suffering in his young life. While those experiences motivated him to pursue a more comfortable life, they also motivated him to teach principles that would help others do more prospering than suffering. Judging not only by his own success, but the accomplishments of many of his students, he has been quite successful.

As his daughter I am most impressed with his spiritual growth and how he adjusts to the many conflicts and challenges he has faced in his later years. I imagine every child would like to see his or her parents experience longevity but it's especially nice to see them in good health. My life is so much better because of my father and I especially give praise and thanks to my Heavenly Father for the beautiful journey I've had thus far. I look forward to the many lessons that life and death will teach me in the future and I hope to observe my grandchildren as they also learn and grow on this earth.

Who knows? Maybe one of my grandchildren will be a pioneer. Seems like pioneers are born into the earth when there is a great need for change and for moving things forward—a Divine appointment, so to speak, to bring a loving and compassionate energy to the planet. They can't fail because they are on a path to successfully bring about the change needed. They have a special role to play in the universal cycle of change.

Sherman Howard learned early in life to recognize the energy of hate and distinguish it from the energy of love.

He used that discernment to educate and dispel the ignorance with excellent endeavors in sports activities and in the school system. He had a Divine assignment as a football player as well as a gym teacher, coach, Athletic Director, father, husband, and all the other roles he has played and continues to play.

We all have a responsibility to change our negative histories as we stay conscious and aware of the harm they have caused. As our President remains optimistic about improving our relationships at home and abroad, we can be the change he campaigned on. Being the change means moving from pessimism to optimism as our inner light prevails and pierces the darkness. We are becoming a collective mind of our Creator, expanding the light within to the true being of non-racial spiritual awareness.

In 1957, Melba Pattillo carried the banner of integration in Little Rock, Arkansas. She and eight other African-American teenagers volunteered to attend segregated Central High and became well known throughout the world as the "Little Rock Nine." As I read her book, *Warriors Don't Cry,* I was moved to tears as I felt the pain she endured for a full school year. Melba's grandmother and mother played a major role in keeping her focused on integration and perhaps more importantly in helping her develop trust and faith in her Heavenly Father's Divine purpose. In a recent interview at Scholastic.com, she spoke eloquently and profoundly about the lesson from her battles:

> I just want to say also, that we all need each other, love is the answer, and that any time you look at another human being, the same God that exists in you, exists in them, and no matter where they came from, who they worship, or what they wear, you owe them eye contact, consideration, and a smile...at the very least.[5]

After a battle like hers, it takes a special heart and deep insight to survive with such compassion still evident. She was born with and has carried the gift of "Oyin," which is the Hebrew word that means "openings of eyes."[6] As with all Hebrew letters and words, however, Oyin also refers to mental and spiritual faculties. I believe we are all born with this gift, but for various reasons that true insight gets blocked and distorted. Enter the messengers and messiahs to help us return to our original, eternal state of mind and heart. As Proverbs 23 reminds us, "He restores our soul" and uses the most interesting humans to cooperate in the work of restoration.

With Barack Obama in the White House, we can truly say we have made progress in tearing down the segregation mentalities, but day-to-day encounters with human emotions give us plenty of opportunities to consider the need for awakening in our fellow human beings. I am filled with gratitude for all the opportunities given to me to smile, make eye contact, and shine a light of love and truth to those struggling with their purpose on this earth. It's all about reaping and sowing, and for sure my father has taught me the most important seeds that bring forth a bountiful harvest are love and compassion. So let's do it. The field is ripe and ready for planting and the earth is in need of a new harvest. Shalom and Namaste!

Sherman and his family, March 2014

****

APPENDIX

Never Be Sick Again: Health is a Choice, Learn How to Choose It by Raymond Francis, Health Communications, Inc. 2002: From 1960 to 2000, obesity among U.S. children aged six to ten years increased 54 percent. Now, an estimated 20 percent of all American children are obese or overweight. Few children outgrow weight problems. Eighty percent of obese children and adolescents become obese adults. These high obesity levels in children are already contributing to cardiovascular disease, diabetes, and cancer. These conditions, now frequently associated with obesity, used to be rare in children.

Nutrition in the Prevention and Treatment of Disease by Ann M. Coulston and Carol J. Boushey, Elsevier, Inc., 2008: Overall, most recent estimates suggest that 17 percent of U.S. children and adolescents are overweight, and an additional 17 percent have a BMI between the 85th and 95th percentiles, indicating a risk of becoming overweight. The high prevalence of obesity among children is of particular concern given that childhood-onset obesity often progresses into adulthood. The alarming increase in the prevalence of obesity during the past few decades has raised concerns about associated health risks for children, adolescents, and adults.

Food Fight by Kelly Brownell and Katherine Battle Horgen, McGraw Hill Companies, Inc. 2004: Obesity in children is a problem of major significance. Rates are growing around the world; the medical, psychological, and social consequences are harsh; and the primary causes, poor diet and declining activity, are growing worse. Obesity in children has increased two- to threefold in the United States in the last twenty-five years. The increase in minority groups is double that in white children.

APPENDIX

The Diabetes Cure: A Natural Plan That Can Slow, Stop, Even Cure Type 2 Diabetes by Dr. Vern Cherewatenko and Paul Perry, Harper Collins Publishers, 1999: Type 2 diabetes is typically associated with obesity, and the latest figures show obesity in children and teens has increased dramatically in recent years.

Footnotes

[1] Read more at Suite101: Shifting Scene: Chicago in 1920s http://www.suite101.com/article.cfm/jazz/71673#ixzz0nM9FKWGa

[2] *Tulsa Tribune*, October 25, 1948.

[3] *My Utmost for His Highest*, The Golden Book of Oswald Chambers, Oswald Chambers Publications Association, Ltd., 1992.

[4] *Ibid*.

[5] Quote from interview at scholastic.com, with Melba Pattillo Beals, one of the nine black teenagers chosen to integrate Central High School in 1957, in Little Rock Arkansas.

[6] www.bethashem.org, *The Dictionary of Torah.*

CONTACT THE AUTHOR

Please email or write the author with any comments you may have. You are also welcome to contact her for bookings. Ms. Robinson is available for book club presentations, book signings, or speaking engagements for your organization.

Contact her at:

Email: viyahta@hotmail.com

Visit her website at:

www.yourholisticlifecoach.com

www.holistichomeandbodycare.com

CPSIA information can be obtained
at www.ICGtesting.com
Printed in the USA
LVOW01s0512141215

466496LV00002B/7/P